PERIOD FLOWER ARRANGING
3000 BC – 1939

AN ESSENTIAL GUIDE

THE NATIONAL ASSOCIATION OF FLOWER ARRANGEMENT SOCIETIES

About NAFAS

'NAFAS' the National Association of Flower Arrangement Societies is an educational charity dedicated to the promotion of the artistic use of all types of plant material through the medium of its flower clubs for both adults and children.

NAFAS is concerned about the environment and members uphold the principles of conservation and preservation of rare and endangered plants and flowers.

With clubs and members throughout the United Kingdom, NAFAS is in a unique position to encourage the art of flower arranging through demonstrations, classes, exhibitions, festivals and show work.

NAFAS is affiliated to the Royal Horticultural Society and is a founder member of the World Association of Floral Artists.

Our mission statement
Sharing the creative use of flowers through education, to bring joy and inspiration to all.

www.nafas.org.uk

Published in 2021 by NAFAS, the National Association of Flower Arrangement Societies
Email: info@nafas.org.uk
www.nafas.org.uk

Copyright © NAFAS 2021

All rights reserved. No part of this publication may be reproduced or transmitted in any form or by any means, electronic or mechanical, including photocopying, recording or any information storage or retrieval system, without prior permission in writing from the publisher

ISBN: 978-0-9542850-6-7

Series Editor: Chloë Bryan-Brown
Design: Amanda Hawkes
Illustrations: John Vagg and Margaret Murray
Cover photograph: Courtesy of the Metropolitan Museum of Art (see credit on page 139)
Printed in Great Britain by Quorum Print Services Ltd, Cheltenham

Contents

Introduction 4
Creating a period arrangement 5

Egyptian 9
Greek and Roman 17
Indian 25
Japanese 35
Chinese 45
Italian Renaissance 53
Tudor 61
Dutch and Flemish 69
American Colonial 77
Georgian 87
Rococo 97
Victorian 105
Edwardian and Art Nouveau 115
The 1920s and 1930s 125

Useful reading 135
Acknowledgements 139

Introduction

This popular guide, first published in 1982, evolved from a successful series of leaflets edited by Daphne Vagg for *Insight*, the Education Journal for Flower Arrangers formerly published by the National Association of Flower Arrangement Societies (NAFAS).

The only available book of its kind, with sections on flower arranging in ancient civilisations around the world as well as specific periods in British history from the Tudors to the 1920s and 1930s, it is a fascinating and useful guide for flower arrangers and an invaluable teaching aid for flower arranging courses. It is widely used for reference and inspiration by students and professional and amateur floral artists, as well as floral art competition judges and floristry and flower arranging educators.

With contributions from well-known names in the history of flower arranging and additional material supplied by Maureen Geddie (Renaissance), Rita Quirk and Lesley Sturdy (Chinese) and members of the NAFAS Education and Judges Committees, this third edition also contains two new comprehensive chapters on Japanese and Indian floral art. Many of the original illustrations by John Vagg are included with new illustrations in the Indian chapter by Margaret Murray.

Plant names

Botanical names for plants have been used throughout the guide to avoid confusion. While common names may be easier to pronounce and remember, botanical names are unique and do not change according to language, dialect or local tradition. Every effort has been made to provide the correct botanical name, but it should be pointed out that even botanical names can change as more is discovered about plants that might result in an update. Botanical names can be cross checked with common names on the RHS website www.rhs.org

Creating a period flower arrangement

Arrangements in period styles may be needed for an exhibition; for decorating stately homes; a recreated period occasion in the theatre; as an examination piece for a course, or for competitive show work. Each of these may call for a slightly different approach, but It is not as difficult as it sounds and you certainly don't have to be an expert. The flower arranger is concerned with creating a period illusion using whatever references available. Here are some hints to help.

Style and atmosphere

A period arrangement interprets the style and character of a particular historical period or artistic style. It can seldom be absolutely authentic but can recreate the atmosphere, line, colour and spirit of a bygone age. The very way in which flowers and leaves are arranged – in a concentric posy, a hand-tied bunch, garland, swag, classical symmetry or swirling asymmetry – will evoke the style typical of a past era.

Colour

Certain colours and colour combinations may be very typical of a period. The Victorians, for example, liked to combine a harsh grassy green with maroon, which perhaps would not be our choice today. Similarly, the Tudor love for bright, mixed colours would contrast with our current preference for subtle toning.

Containers

Obviously, an authentic period container is best if it is available, but many period pieces that we associate with a particular era, such as ewers, bowls and other vessels would not have been used for flowers in their own time. These should be used with discretion. They will lend authenticity to a period arrangement only if the style of the arrangement is suitable. Today, with commercially available replicas, craft materials, books and online tutorials, it is not difficult to imitate a period container – or even create your own.

Mechanics

Unless a period arrangement is especially required as an examination exercise, it is not necessary to use the method for supporting stems (if any), which was actually used in the period concerned. Modern mechanics such as pin holders, wire-netting and water-retaining foams may be used; BUT the use of these mechanics may give a line or a flow which would not have been possible with the period's use of sand, moss, packed cut twigs, glass rose (flower frog) or open mesh cover on a rose bowl. For an authentic look it pays to try out the actual mechanics of the period if known, even if modern mechanics are used for speed and efficiency on the day.

Backgrounds, bases and accessories

These can add to the period atmosphere if well chosen, even if they were not used with flower arrangements at the time. For example, particular fabrics, patterns, decoration, woods, cords, fringes and lace can suggest a period. Even a title card written in a suitable script or style can aid interpretation. Check books or images on the internet for décor and interiors and you will quickly be able to distinguish, for example, Art Nouveau pewter from Tudor or Jacobean items, or the grand scale and exuberance of Baroque compared to the more frivolous Rococo.

Plant materials

As a result of hybridizing, plant material has changed much over the years in variety, colour and size. Generally, flowers are bigger and brighter than they were even 50 years ago. It helps to keep in mind when you are period arranging that:

- smaller flowers are usually more authentic looking
- the use of garden flowers when available is preferable
- long, straight stems are modern while short, curving stems are more typical of period arrangements
- some recent roses, while having all the benefits of a modern rose, retain the delicate charm of old-fashioned roses (e.g., David Austin English Roses)
- substitute flowers of later date, which look similar, should be acceptable as long as the atmosphere created is right e.g., *Lilium longiflorum* for *Lilium candicum*, *Hydrangea* sp. for *Viburnum opulus* 'Roseum', and single spray *Chrysanthemum* cultivars for early introductions of *Chrysanthemum* species.
- except for show work, where artificial plant material is not allowed, it should be acceptable to use good artificial flowers for those which are not available; skilful painting can make even faux flowers quite acceptable if mixed in with fresh flowers

Getting started

In general, flower arrangers are taught to start with an outline of foliage or flowers in bud approximately 1.5 times the height of the container, working in the transitional plant material to a focal point just above the rim of the container. In period arrangements, this well-known routine is rarely possible because the large focal flowers may be at the top; there is little added foliage and the sheer variety of flowers makes it difficult to control the design to give it cohesion and rhythm. The colours may be hard to balance, and proportions different.

A good exercise is to reproduce an Old Master in real plant material because it makes you look carefully at the overall composition and each flower, leaf and stem to appreciate the proportions, colour, balance, creation of depth and balance at the top and at the base. There will be the problem of translating a two-dimensional painting into a three-dimensional fact which forces you to analyse the features and design principles in a picture and to apply them.

Egyptian
3000 BC – 332 BC

JANE NEATBY

The history of Ancient Egypt began when Upper and Lower Egypt were united under a single ruler about 3000 BC and ended when it was absorbed into Alexander's empire in 332 BC.

Sometimes called the 'gift of the Nile', it was one of the oldest and most enduring of all civilisations with a highly organised state of government that came into being well before 3000 BC. The reason for such early efficiency was the need to oversee the many thousands of workers required to manage the annual flooding of the River Nile, which enriched the surrounding land with a thick layer of fertile soil while the higher ground remained desert.

Social structure changed little in the period. Men and woman appear to have been theoretically equal in law, and high and low were entitled to their subsistence (bread and beer) from the pharaoh, who was the centre of the distribution of land, power and goods.

Religious belief was mainly that of an agricultural people with fertility gods, resurrection and eternal life. The philosophy of *maat*, or truth, and the unchanging order of life was the basis of Egyptian attitudes, which gave a static quality to art and religious customs. Happy and laughter-loving, living life to the full, their essential aim was to extend that life, unchanged, through all the ages of eternity. Their tombs were built in their lifetime and filled with artefacts and treasures, the walls painted with scenes from daily life, moments of joy, honour, work and recreation to be used or re-enacted in the 'other world'.

Not being a particularly war-like people, they conquered through trade and good government and, being tolerant in religious matters, made no concerted effort to spread their culture. Although Egyptian wealth and power influenced many lands, Egypt was little changed by increasing contact with the outside world until the Alexandrian conquest in 332 BC.

Tombs, temples and hieroglyphs remained to mystify and delight the world. The astonishing accomplishments of pyramid and monumental art lived on, but the so-called 'Eternal Egypt' was eternal no more.

How and where flowers were used

While there is evidence for the Egyptians' love of flowers and their constant use in daily life for personal adornment, as gifts, in ritual and funerary offerings and simply for sheer delight in their beauty, there is nothing to indicate that flowers were arranged in the home.

Up to the Fifth Dynasty (2480 BC), flowers are rarely seen as decoration in daily life. From then on, scarcely an eating table or still-life is without a *Nymphaea caerulea* (lotus) or anyone without a flower to their nose, in their hair, over their arm or around their neck. On tomb paintings, there is evidence of:

- *Nymphaea caerulea* flowers curved around jars with no visible means of support
- borders in garland form, with individual flowers hanging vertically from the band which holds them
- garlands of mixed flowers with leaves used on alternate sides (giving the effect of silver on green) were presented to the living and dead
- simple tight posies, or single flowers in woven or metal holders
- offering tables, vases and trays piled high with fruit, vegetables and flowers
- staff-shaped bundles often the height of a man

At funeral ceremonies, collarettes were worn, made from a backing of *Cyperus papyrus*, with beads, *Nymphaea caerulea*, *Centaurea cyanus*, berries, slices of *Mandragora officinarum* and leaves of *Salix* sp., *Olea europaea* and *Phoenix dactylifera*.

Tomb scene showing collarettes made from plant material and flowers in a holder (illustration inspired by Tomb of Nebamun at the British Museum, London)

Typical settings

- temples, tombs and pyramids made for eternity, built of hard-stone or rock
- houses built of wood, mud-brick and reeds
- interiors, brightly painted or hung with painted hangings of scenes from nature
- floors, tiled or painted with scenes of lakes with birds, fish and water plants
- ceilings often painted to resemble the sky
- well-made furniture of good simple design, often with plant motifs
- clothes were stored in boxes brightly painted with flowers of *Nymphaea caerulea*, *Cyperus papyrus* and geometric patterns
- meals were served on trays on stands
- tableware was elegant and colourful – for the wealthy, magnificent services of gold and silver

Overall characteristics of the period

- Paintings and carvings show a highly stylized, rigid and symmetrical manner of placing plant material, often in threes or in pairs.

- When using in threes, the largest flower is placed at the top centre with two buds or opening flowers slightly below, on either side of the central stem. In tall arrangements such as the ceremonial staffs, the largest flowers are at the top and fruit alternate with flowers in a stiff ascending line on either side of the central stem.

- Flowers appear to be placed mainly to show the side view, with little or no added foliage.

- Apparently, little or no attempt was made to prolong the life of the plant by placing stems in water.

Typical backgrounds

- marsh or river scenes, blue skies, palm tree, sunsets
- abrupt landscape contrasts; rich fertile to harsh desert scenes
- pyramids and sphinxes; sand
- black hieroglyphs on brick red ground
- pleated linen
- squatting figures of the gods or godlings
- columns with *Nymphaea caerulea* or *Cyperus papyrus* capitols

Egyptian hieroglyphs were the formal writing system used in Ancient Egypt

Papyrus-shaped columns at the Temple of Karnak, Luxor

Colour

Areas of colour in paintings are in clear hues, usually without any modification into tints, tones and shades. Some of the more frequently used colours were dark blue, turquoise blue, green, gold, black, rose, brick-red.

Green symbolised fertility and was the colour of the god Osiris
Black symbolised eternity and was the colour of the god Anubis
Red symbolised evil and was the colour of the god Seth

The traditional colour of the clothes seen in tomb paintings is white. Other colours were worn, dyes being obtained from a variety of plants and molluscs. Headbands and chaplets were mainly blue, white and rose and garlands and posies were polychromatic.

In statuary, men were painted red-brown; women, pale yellow.

Containers

The ingrained conservatism of the Egyptians and the limitations of the magico-religious approach tended inevitably to inhibit innovation. Forbidden as they were by law and religious custom to change the style and usages of their predecessors, their individual art in all its forms, remained little changed over a period of 3,000 years.

In a country rich in gold and silver and electrum (a natural alloy of gold and silver), the art of the goldsmith flourished. The use of silver was comparatively rare since its value was much greater than gold.

Graceful vessels were made in precious and base metals. The beautiful material known as Egyptian faience, which is not a true faience but an alkaline glazed quartz frit, was widely used for bowls and chalices.

Glass, although known, was not greatly used until the New Kingdom when it enjoyed a certain vogue. However, the popularity of glass declined with the development of a new material 'glassy faience'.

The Ancient Egyptians had, in prehistoric times, already created a good number of forms. They fashioned vases not only in pottery but, using methods which seem incredible today, carved them out of stone, although less difficult materials such as alabaster and serpentine were used.

Containers in a variety of forms could be made from precious and base metals, Egyptian faience, pottery, carved stone or basket work

Simple woven baskets and wooden trays, often banded with gold, were also used, and poke- shaped containers are frequently seen holding bunched posies of mixed flowers or a stylized arrangement of lotus and papyrus.

The overall style of containers showed grace and restraint until the Ptolemaic period (330–30 BC).

Suggested accessories

- the ankh symbol
- painted cut-out boats and mummy cases (usually available from the British Museum shop)
- bowls or vases of corn seed or fruits
- boxes painted with hieroglyphs and geometric patterns.
- striped glass fish, copies of which can be found in gift shops
- figures of gods made from modelling clay or polystyrene and suitably painted
- ointment jars and bottles painted in the Egyptian style
- ushabti figures painted pale blue with black detail

The ankh was a symbol of eternal life

Ushabti figure were funerary figurines used in tombs to carry out tasks for the deceased in the afterlife

References and resources

Plant material

The variety of plant material used in funeral wreaths, garlands and posies between 3000–1500 BC is strong evidence that plants not indigenous to Egypt were being increasingly brought in as part of tribute, trade and botanical expedition.

Acacia sp.
Acanthus sp.
Allium ampeloprasum var. *porrum*
Allium cepa
Allium sativum
Aloe sp.
Anemone sp.
Artemesia absinthium
Boxwellia carterii
Centaura cyanus
Commiphora abyssinica
Cucumis sativus
Cucurbita pepo
Cuminum cyminum
Cyperus papyrus
Ficus sycomorus
Hedera sp.
Jasminum sp.
Juncus sp.
Lactuca sativa
Lagenaria vulgaris
Lathyrus sativus
Laurus sp.
Lawsonia inermis
Lilium sp.
Lupinus sp.
Malva sp.
Mandragora officinarum
Mentha sp.
Myosotis sp.
Myrtus communis
Narcissus tazetta
Nardostachys jatamansi
Nymphaea caerulea
Olea europaea
Papaver sp.
Phoenix dactylifera
Phragmites communis
Punica granatum
Ranunculus sp.
Ribes sanguineum
Ricinus communis
Salix sp.
Solanum dulcamara
Tamarix mannifera
Viola odorata
Vitis vinifera
Xerochrysum sp. (syn. *Helichrysum*)

Places to see

Museums and galleries

Ashmolean Museum (Oxford)

British Museum (London), the country's most important Egyptian collection

The Fitzwilliam Museum (Cambridge)

University College Department of Egyptology Museum (London)

Historic buildings and monuments

Chiddingstone Castle (Kent)

Cleopatra's Needle (London)

Greek and Roman

Greek 600–146 BC · Roman AD 28–325

CHRISTINE PEER

The Greek and Roman civilisations were similar in many respects, not least the climate and the flora. Their calendars were a sequence of religious and civic festivals, and both enjoyed sport and outdoor activities. The Romans admired the Greek culture, architecture and sculpture, and 'borrowed' their gods, many of whom they renamed.

The Greeks were philosophical and appreciated beauty in all its forms. Their use of plant material was mainly to honour gods and heroes, and to bring atmosphere, rest and relaxation to their garden courtyards. The Romans were a more practical people and great gardeners who spread the art of gardening throughout their empire and brought it to Britain.

The Greek civilisation was, of course, pre-Christian but, during the era of the Roman Empire, Christianity was spreading and becoming a strong influence.

How and where flowers were used

There is little evidence to show if the Greeks or the Romans displayed cut flowers in vases, though they do appear to have used cut leafy branches, possibly *Myrtus communis*, in tall pedestal containers and vases as part of wedding preparations. These probably had religious significance. Plants were also grown decoratively in vases and pots in garden courtyards.

Figures from a Greek thigh guard decoration showing cut leafy branches in tall containers, fifth century BC

Baskets and cornucopias

Flowers and fruit were certainly collected in baskets and cornucopias. A Roman mosaic of the second century AD suggests that they were also arranged in shallow wicker baskets or *canistra*. A wall painting at Pompeii shows three women putting flowers in tall baskets but it is not clear if they are just collecting, or actually arranging the flowers.

Wreaths and garlands

These forms of decoration were extensively used by both Greeks and Romans, and this was by far the most popular way of using cut plant material. Wreaths were made by sewing plant material together or by twining stems, such as *Ficus carica*, which is mentioned by the Greek philosopher Theophrastus. Garland-makers were the florists of the day. One, named Glycera, was famous throughout Greece for her wreaths and garlands, and a fresco in the House of Vetti at Pompeii shows cherubs making and selling garlands of flowers.

Garland makers

Wreaths and chaplets were worn on the head and garlands hung around the neck or over one shoulder and across the breast. They were made of leaves alone, or of flowers and leaves, or with nuts, fruits and cereals added, often with cords and ribbons intertwined. Some examples of the types of chaplets include:

Corona civica made of leaves and fruits of *Quercus* sp., a mark of great honour.

Corona radiata resembling a crown and given to gods and deified heroes.

Corona natalitia usually of *Hedera* sp., *Laurus* sp., or *Petroselinum crispum* hung over the doors in the home of a new baby.

Corymbus a wreath of leaves with fruits of *Hedera* sp. and edible fruit to decorate statues, especially of Dionysus/Bacchus.

Encarpa a swag of fruit and flowers used for decoration in sculpture or painting.

Serta a mixed flower garland used to decorate houses, temples and altars at festival times.

Encarpa

Guests at feasts and games wore coronets of *Agrostemma githago*; magistrates and Olympic Games' winners in Greece, and poets and playwrights in Rome, wore *Myrtus communis*; victors in war or sport were honoured with *Laurus nobilis* as were academics, hence our word baccalaureate. Roman crown garlands or chaplets were tied at the back of the head with ribbons (*taenia*) allowed to hang loose down the back.

Coin showing crown garland and ribbon

Strewn flowers

Flowers and petals were cast on streets, lakes, floors, tables and beds on festive and ceremonial occasions. Emperor Nero's vast and luxurious Golden House palace had a revolving ceiling to scatter flowers over the guests. Another emperor is said to have let so many petals fall from the ceiling of his imperial dining room that his guests were suffocated under their weight.

The *thyrsus*

A tall slim staff was carried at festivals of Dionysus/Bacchus. This *thyrsus* was entwined with ivy and surmounted with a pine cone from the ancient Greek custom of flavouring wine with pine resin. The staff was often decorated with leaves, berries, grapes and ribbons and can be seen in many Greek and Roman paintings.

Flowers in scarves

The author Margaret Marcus (*Period Flower Arrangement*, Barrows, 1952) records that the Romans added the blossom-filled scarf to the Greek floral traditions. The scarf was held in both hands across the body like an apron and used to carry flowers and fruit to religious ceremonies. A large marble urn from Pompeii at the 1976 London exhibition 'Pompeii AD 79' showed this.

A thyrsus

Typical settings

- marbles of various colours and markings, white, yellow, green and white, red, black and red, and purple with cream
- silvery-grey limestone and warm yellow sandstone
- floors of pictorial and geometric mosaics, often in black and white, as can be seen at Fishbourne Roman Palace and at Bignor Roman Villa (West Sussex)
- columns in Corinthian, Doric and Ionic styles
- *Acanthus* leaf, stylised *Lonicera* and Greek-key motif
- brilliantly coloured frescoes, especially portraying the legends of the gods
- courtyard gardens with colonnaded walks
- low stone or marble benches
- outdoor vistas, a reminder of the largely open-air life in Mediterranean countries – the tall dark cypress tree is typical in Greece, natural countryside groves, often sacred shrines to gods

Symbolism

- Most uses of flowers, fruit and foliage were ritualistic as offerings to the gods, either to placate or please them, or to ask for favours and blessings. Important gods had specific plants associated with them; for example: Zeus/Jupiter – *Quercus*; Apollo – *Laurus*; Athene/Minerva – *Olea*; Aphrodite/Venus – *Myrtus*; Dionysys/Bacchus – *Hedera* and *Vitis*; Demeter/Ceres – *Papaver*.
- The wreath was a symbol of eternity and rebirth. The plant material used in wreaths and garlands was often used for its supposed medicinal qualities as well as ritualistic purposes.
- Roses were used to stuff mattresses and pillows, from which practice comes the saying 'a bed of roses'.
- Athens has been called the 'violet-crowned' city.
- Lovers' poems are full of symbolic references to plants to be used in garlands for the beloved.

Overall characteristics of the period

The styles of the two cultures are really very similar so far as the flower arranger is concerned, but that of the Romans was heavier, more elaborate and more ornate, especially in the later decadent decline of the Roman Empire. Nonetheless, we still speak of the classical simplicity of these eras, and they have never been superseded in their use of good proportions, perfect balance and overall harmony of design.

Colour

These were more colourful eras than is generally realised. Interiors had painted walls and frescoes and, in Roman Pompeii, walls were painted in dark greens, black, golden beige and rich Pompeian red. Brides wore saffron-coloured robes and orange veils, and imperial purple was used by the Roman emperors. Statuary was often painted in bright naturalistic colours to show facial features, robes and ornaments.

Flowers were of cheerful, varied colours, often mixed together. "... there are chaplets of violet blossoms mixed with saffron, and yellow garlands blended with crimson roses" (attributed to Virgil, 70–19 BC).

Containers

- baskets, both the large flat wicker basket without handles – *canistra* – and tall beaker-shaped baskets, again without handles – *calathos*
- cornucopia, originally a drinking horn, but later of wicker, metal or even stone, the symbol of plenty
- tall decorated vases used by the Greeks in wedding celebrations

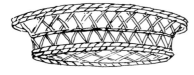

Canistrum

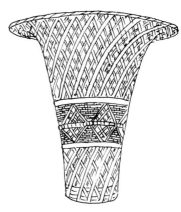

Calathos

GREEK AND ROMAN

Suggested accessories

- vases, urns, *kraters* (large bowls for mixing wine and water), *hydria* (water jars), *kantharos* (drinking cups) and *ampohorae* (storage jars)
- terracotta and other clay bowls
- writing scrolls on wooden reels
- columns in marble and stone
- coloured glass goblets and jugs in black with white marbling, blue and amber (Roman)
- oil lamps in bronze or terracotta
- braziers or lamp stands on three legs with animal feet
- gold, silver, brass and copper coins showing garlanded heads
- incised lettering on stone and marble slabs
- classical statues or statuettes, especially of the human figure, but also of birds and beasts

Kantharos

Amphora

Hydria

Bronze stand

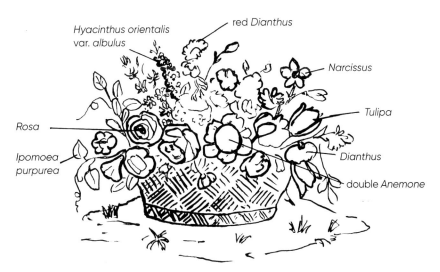

Illustration from a second century Roman mosaic showing a shallow basket with typical plant material

References and resources

Plant material

Flowers	Foliage	Edible fruits	Vegetables
Agrostemma githago	*Acanthus* sp.	apple	beetroot
Anemone sp.	*Buxus* sp.	cereals	celery
Asphodelus sp.	*Cupressus* sp.	cherry	cruciferous vegetables
Calendula sp.	*Fagus* sp.	citrus fruit	endive
Centaurea cyanus	*Hedera* sp. & fruits	date	fennel
Crocus sativas	*Laurus* sp.	fig	leek
Delphinium sp.	*Laurus nobilis*	grape	lettuce
Erica sp.	*Mentha* sp.	hazelnut	onion
Helleborus sp.	*Myrtus communis*	medlar	species of beans
Hyacinthus orientalis	*Nerium oleander*	melon	West Indian gherkin
Iris sp.	*Phoenix dactylifera*	mulberry	
Lilium sp.	*Quercus* sp.	olive	
Lonicera sp.	*Salix* sp.	peach	
Narcissus sp.	*Salvia* sp.	pear	
Papaver sp.	*Salvia rosmarinus*	plum	
Rosa sp.	*Taxus baccata*	pomegranate	
Tulip sp.	*Thymus* sp.	quince	
Viola odorata	*Vitis* sp.	walnut	

Places to see

Museums and galleries

The British Museum (London), has many items of interest and many local museums up and down the country house 'finds' from the Roman occupation.

Places

Roman remains are still to be seen in Britain and can provide background knowledge. For example, in Bath (Somerset), St. Albans (Hertfordshire), Fishbourne (West Sussex), Bignor (West Sussex), Lullingstone (Kent), Pompeii (Italy) and Herculaneum (Italy).

People to look up

Writers

Dioscorides (AD 40–90) a physician/botanist who wrote *De Materia Medica*

Pliny the Elder (AD 23–79) who wrote *Historia Naturalis* a full account of the gardens and plants of his day

Pliny the Younger (AD 62–116) his letters give much information about Roman Gardens

Theophrastus (372–287 BC) philosopher who wrote *Historia Plantarum* and *De Causis Plantarum*

Virgil (70–19 BC) Roman epic poet

Indian
100BC – Current day

VALERIE BEST

The history of Indian floral design is rich in cultural and religious connections and can be traced back to earliest times. A stone carving held in the Government Museum in Chennai dated from 100 BC depicts a perfectly symmetrical stylised arrangement of *Nelumbo nucifera* (lotus) flowers and seed pods in a container.

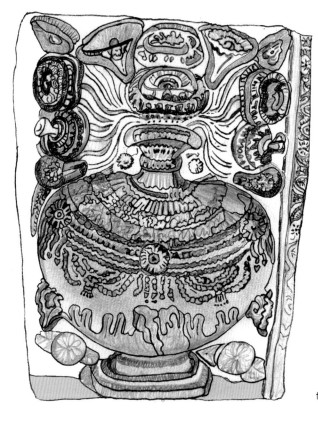

Stone carving of an early flower arrangement with flowers and seed pods

Nature was worshipped and revered. The Sanskrit word *puja* or worship originated from the Dravidian term *pu* denoting a ritual in which the main offerings are flowers, leaves and fruits while the Bhagavad Gita Hindu scripture states that leaves, flowers, fruits and water offered with love are most readily accepted by the Lord.

Ways were also found to make the infinite into a finite being that could be seen and touched. The *purna kalash* was one such creation – an earthenware pot with the base shaped to represent a human torso while the upper portion was decorated with at least five, and up to nine, different kinds of leaves, a coconut and a bright vibrant flower at the crown. The finished creation represents the combination of nature, the elements and man. They were carried by people on their travels, including monks passing along the Silk Road to Japan, where they would be placed on temple altars and later in homes, where they became the precursors to *Ikebana*.

Purna kalash

Indian history is a kaleidoscope of foreign invaders and rulers and floral design has inevitably been influenced by various traditions including the Mughuls from 1526, who brought narrow-necked vases and two-tier arrangements with the addition of a small, lower bowl for fruits. Such vases were kept in niches and on trays with a decanter and glass and also used in displays when serving food seated on carpets; floral floor decorations also became popular for special occasions.

International trade brought with it new commodities and plants. In 1820, the English Christian missionary William Carey founded the Agricultural and Horticultural Society of India, which was to have a huge influence on gardens and the plant trade.

Narrow-necked vase in the Mughul style

How and where flowers were used

Since the earliest days of civilisation, tribal people who settled mainly in northern India used flowers and plants profusely for folk festivals, religious ceremonies, public celebrations, weddings and courtship. The majority of these events, because of the climate, took place outside rather than in the house.

Flowers were also an integral part of the cultural embellishment of women. In the fourth century AD, Vatsyayana, author of the *Kama Sutra*, laid down that an accomplished lady was considered to be one who had acquired 64 types of art, of which floral art was an important one.

More generally, flowers were and are used widely for:

- cultural and religious events, festivals
- daily decoration of temples
- decoration of homes (usually outside before the 19th century)
- personal adornment: floral jewellery, hand and hair decorations
- hanging decorations
- floor decorations: *alpana* and *rangoli* designs

Patterns for alpana and rangoli floor decorations

Garlands

Brightly coloured flower garlands have long been popular with India's many different communities. Symbolising purity, honour, goodwill, love and beauty, they serve as religious offerings and are used in domestic rituals and public ceremonies either worn by individuals or to decorate temples, pillars or even trees. Stringing them requires patience and vibrant and scented flowers are preferred including *Nerine*, *Plumeria*, *Thespesia populnea*, *Jasminum*, *Tagetes* and *Dianthus*.

Typical settings

- outside or in temples and niches as religious offerings
- floor designs along with trays of food also decorated with flowers and plants
- on tables, particularly low tables for special events (not usually inside before the 19th century)
- draped in garlands on bamboo and fabric screens and as a backdrop for occasions

Symbolism

All Indian floral art is influenced by its extensive history and religious symbolism which is based on:

- Om, the sound of creation
- creation, the union of male and female
- nature, flowers, leaves, fruit, vegetables
- religion and festivals
- music and dance
- freedom, peace and enlightenment

Om symbol

Indian dance gestures can express symbolic meaning

Plant symbolism

At weddings, garlands of flowers symbolise the union of two souls as well as the fragility of life and human feelings. Flowers with particular symbolism include:

Rosa symbol of God
Narcissus an eye of a devotee of God
Viola, **Lilium** and **Jasminum** various facial features of a devotee
Tulipa a wine cup

Overall characteristics of the period

- All Indian art forms are based on ideas or mood; therefore, it is not so much the form of the flowers but the expression of an idea that guides the arrangements.
- Floral garlands, floor decorations and special decorations for festivals and special occasions such as wedding nights were more common than flowers in a vase.
- Often designs used multiple colours and flowers.
- By the end of the 19th century, Western style arrangements in a vase were common for public displays while Indian styles were retained for rituals and religious ceremonies.
- Latterly, after the Second World War, Indian design was also influenced by Ikebana.

Colour

Colour is everywhere in India. Bright colours in particular are frequently seen including red, white, orange, and green, also yellow.

Containers

- earthenware pots, brass/copper bowls, baskets, wooden and pottery trays
- narrow-necked, slim vases, often on a dish
- any large vessels for water
- terracotta pots and jugs

INDIAN 31

Various container shapes

Mechanics

- flowers placed loosely in vases or in low bowls supported by leaves and fruit
- for wider neck vases, groups of twigs and leaves wedged together to support stems
- sand, stones, small pieces of driftwood, twine
- tall, slim-necked vases required no mechanics to support one or two stems

Suggested accessories

- lamps, bamboo mats and trays, musical instruments, ornaments, decanters, kitchen utensils
- hair decorations
- figures of gods/goddesses, pictures from religious texts and books
- fabrics embroidered with flowers and paisley patterns (the paisley teardrop/tadpole shape was introduced by the Mughals from Central Asia

Fabrics with the paisley pattern

Some popular Indian musical instruments

INDIAN 33

Lamps and decorative containers

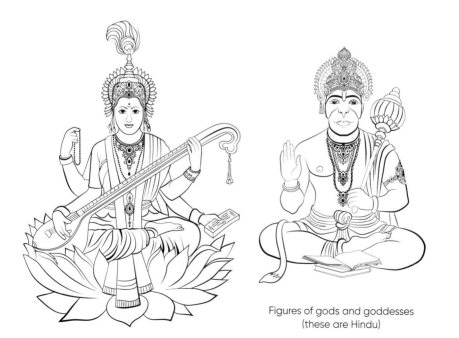

Figures of gods and goddesses
(these are Hindu)

References and resources

Plant material

Aeschynomene sp.
Azadirachta indica
Calendula officinalis
Cassia fistula
Cocos nucifera
Corchorus capsularis
Delonix regia
Ficus benghalensis
Jasminum officinale
Lilium sp.
Musa acuminata
Narcissus sp.
Nelumbo nucifera
Ocimum tenuiflorum
Paeonia sp.
Rosa sp.
Santalum album
Saraca indica
Tagetes
Tecoma stans
Thevetia peruviana
Vinca major

Places to see

Museums and galleries

British Museum (London)

V&A Museum (London)

Historic buildings and monuments

Royal Pavilion, Brighton (East Sussex)

Sezincote House & Gardens (Gloucestershire)

Gardens

BAPS Shri Swaminayran Mandir temple gardens (London)

Japanese
594–1860

DAPHNE VAGG

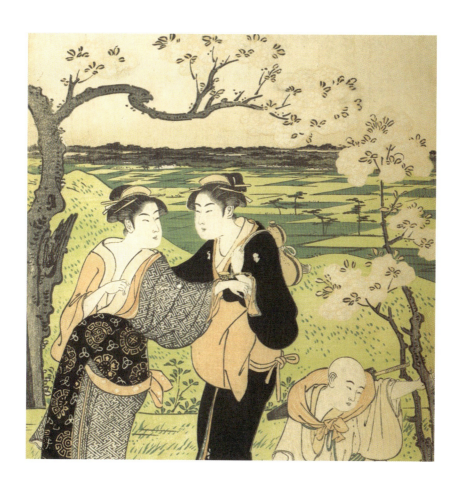

Japanese flower arrangement – *Ikebana*, which means 'living flowers', 'creating with flowers' or 'the way or path of flowers', dates from the sixth century when Chinese priests took Buddhism to Japan and, with it, the custom of offering the Buddha flowers.

For all its apparent simplicity, it is exceedingly complex and steeped in tradition, ritual and symbolism. Its roots are in Shinto, the ancient, indigenous, nature-worshipping, religion of Japan, Buddhism, with its practice of making offerings of flowers, incense, and fire or light (as candles) and Zen philosophy with its simplifying influences of restraint and understatement. Initially, because Buddhism is dedicated to the preservation of life in all its forms, offerings of *Nelumbo nucifera* flowers and leaves were placed in vases of water to prolong their life, and so Japanese flower arrangement began, known in this form as *Tatebana* or 'standing' or 'upright' flowers.

Early in the seventh century, a Japanese nobleman, Ono-no-Imoko, visited China where, believing that flowers for the Buddha should be carefully and thoughtfully displayed, he learnt the first formal method of displaying different plant materials in one container. This style became known as *Rikka*. Ono-no-Imoko went on to found the first classical school of Ikebana, the Ikenobo School. It is still the most popular school of Ikebana in Japan today.

For almost 800 years, Ikebana continued as a devotional offering in temples and palaces, carried out by priests, court attendants and samurai warriors. Women did not become involved until the end of the 19th century.

From the 13th century onwards, the growing influence of Zen philosophy developed into Zen-Buddhism, bringing simplicity, restraint and 'saying more with less' to the previous elaborate, formal and ostentatious display of the temple and court styles. In the 15th century, interest in the arts became more widespread and was eventually taken up by ordinary people. To suit their smaller homes, a smaller, simpler form of flowers for the tea ceremony known as *Chabana* developed and an even simpler, more natural and informal style called *Nageire*, or 'thrown in'.

Interest in Ikebana has spread in the West, where it has influenced freestyle and abstract flower arranging.

Typical settings

In temples and palaces, you would find large Rikka arrangements.

In the home, an essential feature was a room with an alcove for domestic worship known as a *tokonoma*. A scroll picture or poem was hung in the alcove with an ikebana design to the side. There might also be one art object – good taste would not permit more.

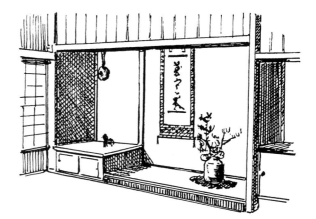

Tokonoma featuring a scroll and floral arrangement

The tea ceremony (*chado* or *cha-no-yu*) also involved Ikebana. Dating from the second century, at a time of lavish and ostentatious display, the tea ceremony, which combines the appreciation of beautiful objects with the act of serving others, was later simplified. Water is boiled and green tea (*matcha*) made and offered to guests in a series of traditional, ritualistic movements. The guests sip the tea and admire the utensils and the scroll and flowers in the tokonoma.

Symbolism

The important concept of the balance of opposite or complementary forces in nature and the universe is usually expressed by the symbol known as *In* or *Yo* (similar to *Yin* and *Yang* in Chinese).

In is female, night, dark, shade, the underside of leaves, flower buds, grasses, white, blue, green and yellow colours.

Yo is male, light, day, sun, the upper side of leaves, pink/red/orange colours, trees and full open flowers.

In Yo symbol

As Ikebana is traditionally asymmetrical, each arrangement has its In and Yo sides; with about 30% on the lighter, more open In side and around 70% on the heavier, denser Yo side.

The plant material itself is also heavy with symbolism, much of it centuries old.

Nelumbo nucifera is sacred to Buddha.
Ipomoea purpurea symbolises the transiency of life.
Prunus persica is associated with children.
Paeonia represents wealth and prosperity.
Pinus is for constancy (used for weddings).
Prunus domestica symbolises purity, sweetness, tender sorrow and virtue.
Wisteria is the gentleness and devotion of Japanese women; the transition from spring to summer.
Eternal youth is symbolised by *Pinus* with *Rosa* or *Paeonia; Celaginella, Pinus* and *Rohdea japonica*.
The seven flowers of autumn are *Dianthus, Eupatorium purpureum, Lespedeza thunbergia, Miscanthus, Patrinia, Platycodon grandiflorus, Pueraria*.
The three friends of winter are bamboo, *Pinus* and *Prunus domestica*, together symbolising steadfastness, perseverance and resilience.

Overall characteristics of the period

All traditional Ikebana is asymmetrical and three dimensional.

It is customary with pictures of Ikebana to have diagrams of the main placements in elevation and bird's-eye view to show the comparative stem lengths and three-dimensional details of angles and directions.

The tallest, strongest stem is the first to go in. Often called *shin* and generally held to represent heaven, it is calculated as the height plus the diameter of the container, multiplied by 1.5 or two. The second longest, often called *soe*, representing man, is 0.65–0.75 the length of shin. The third main line, often called *hikae*, represents Earth, and is 0.5–0.75 the length of soe. These proportions relate to the length of stem seen <u>above</u> the container. The main lines are placed in the arrangement first and in that order.

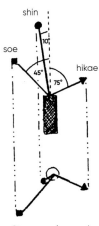

Stem angles and directions

The prescribed angles between the stems and how they rise from the container are shown in the diagram.

Cutting and trimming of side branches, twigs and leaves is far more important in Ikebana than it is in Western arranging. The aim is to create a pleasing line or grouping – one that is asymmetric and irregular, yet graceful and interesting – and to create space.

The container is always part-filled with water before starting to arrange. This helps to weight it and ensure that the stems go straight into water.

A bowl of water (a cutting bowl) is always to hand so all stems are cut under water to prevent airlocks.

Particular characteristics

Rikka is the oldest formal style. Developed from Tatebana, the original temple style, it is built rather than arranged, using originally seven and now nine 'functional lines' or placements representing aspects of the natural landscape and the beauty and harmony of nature – for example, the high peak, hill, waterfall, valley, village and water's edge. Over the centuries, the individual lines and their precise placement and angles have changed, but the diagram gives the current accepted names and positions of the main components. It is an important feature of Rikka that all stems rise as one from the container typifying the unity of nature.

17th century
Rikka design

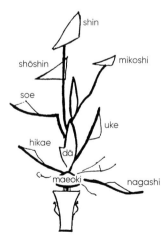

Current accepted names and positions of the main components in a Rikka design

Rikka was too large and too complicated for the tokonoma so a smaller style, influenced by the simplicity and austerity of Zen, developed. Called *Seika* or *Shoka*, it was still mainly formal and selected and emphasised the three important lines of heaven, man and earth. In traditional arrangements, usually only one type of plant material was used for the three lines. If this material was non-flowering, then flowers were added. Some arrangements were made with flowers and their leaves only, for example, *Iris, Narcissus, Paeonia* and *Chrysanthemum*.

Seika/Shoka

At first there were very few regulations but, by the 18th century, precise rules had been imposed, creating some rigidity. One or two types of plant material could then be used but the three main lines still rose as one from the container.

Meanwhile, the growing popularity of the tea ceremony and the continuing influence of Zen-Buddhism meant that an even simpler, quite informal flower arrangement style was needed to complement the ceremony. Called *Chabana*, these tea ceremony flowers appeared natural and uncontrived. Usually, only one or two types of flowers or leaves were used, and preferably those of a light hue, for example, *Iris* in a bamboo container, a single *Prunus persica* blossom in a basket or a *Chrysanthemum* in a pottery vase. The arrangement was intended to suggest a poetic mood of remoteness and contemplation.

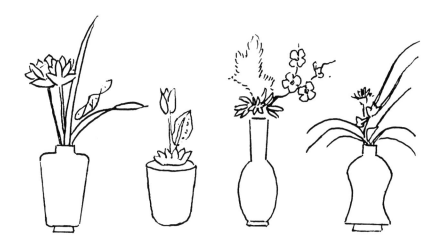

Simple 16th and 17th century Chabana arrangements for the tea ceremony

Nageire ('thrown in') styles conformed to some rules but, from the 15th century, they were an informal alternative to the rigid formality of Rikka and Seika/Shoka. The whole arrangement was less luxurious but the 'heaven-man-earth' lines were still stressed, though more loosely and with possible variations.

Nageire

Colour

It is difficult to be precise about the ancient Japanese attitude to colour in flower arrangements. The overall impression is that it was of comparatively little significance since classical Rikka did not generally use many flowers. Shape, line angle and symbolism were of much greater importance.

Containers

Rikka Tall and heavy, originally bronze in trumpet or urn shapes; was used later, celandon (pale green glazed pottery), porcelain, bamboo and baskets.

Seika/Shoka Bronze was used as in Rikka, but also porcelain, matt glazed pottery, cylinders of bamboo and hanging containers of wood or bamboo.

Chabana Simple pottery, narrow necked vases and cylinders and bamboo baskets seen. Porcelain and bronze are seldom used, nor is glass. There may be some simple surface decoration, but strongly patterned containers are not employed.

Nageire The choice was virtually unlimited, the only criterion being that it should be suitable for the setting and for the plant material chosen. Usually taller rather than wide, they could be porcelain, pottery, glass, wood, basketry or metal.

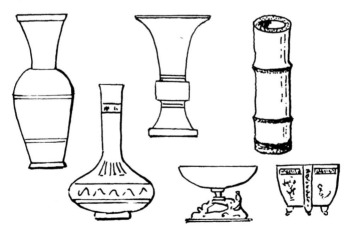

Selection of container styles

Mechanics

Rikka The support for a Rikka is a straw base made to fit the container and firmly wedged in. A number of small straw bundles are tied together tightly with string in the centre and at the bottom, but more loosely at the top to allow stems to be pushed in and firmly held.

Seika or Shoka The mechanics for these are known as *kubari*, wooden sticks which support stems in tall narrow containers. There were several different types of these ranging from vertical to cross-bar and single-bar.

Suna-no-mono ('sand things') In the 15th and 16th centuries, a form of Rikka developed which was arranged in a shallow container (*sunabachi* or *suiban*) filled with sand or small pebbles. The width always exceeded the height in this style.

Chabana If support is needed, *kubari*, are used.

Selection of mechanics

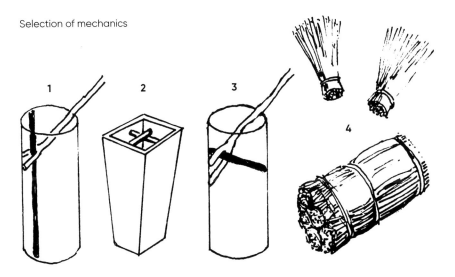

Kubari: 1 vertical fixture, 2 cross-bar, 3 single-bar   4 Straw base for Rikka

Suggested accessories

In the tokonoma at home, there may be a scroll picture, or poem; there might also be one *objet d'art*, good taste would not permit more.

References and resources

Plant material

Flowers
Astilbe
Azalea
Camellia
Chrysanthemum
Celosia argentea
Cydonia oblonga (blossom and fruit)
Cytisus scoparius
Dianthus
Eriobotrya japonica
Forsythia
Gardenia
Hemerocallis (yellow),
Hosta
Hydrangea
Ipomoea purpurea
Iris sp.
Lilium longiflorum
Magnolia sp.
Malva
Malus
Nandina
Narcissus
Nelumbo nucifera
Nymphaea
Orchid sp.
Paeonia
Papaver
Prunus sp. (P. armeniaca, P. domestica, P. persica)
Punica granatum (blossom and fruit)
Pyrus
Salix caprea
Wisteria

Foliage
Acer palmatum
Aspidistra
Bamboo sp.
Buxus
Cedrus
Cryptomeria
Cupressus
Grass sp.
Ilex crenata
Juniperus
Nandina
Pinus
Reed sp.
Rhododendron
Salix babylonica
Taxus baccata

Flowers of the month

January bamboo, *Pinus, Prunus, Narcissus*

February *Prunus domestica*

March *Prunus persica, Camellia, Salix*

April *Prunus* (flowering cherry), *Daphne, Magnolia, Primula*

May *Azalea, Iris, Paeonia, Wisteria*

June *Paeonia, Lilium*

July *Hydrangea, Nelumbo nucifera, Lilium*

August *Ipomoea purpurea*

September gourd, seven flowers of autumn, *Chrysanthemum*

October fruit, particularly persimmon

November *Chrysanthemum, Acer palmatum* leaves

December bamboo, berried branches, *Camellia*

Places to see

Gardens

There are many inspirational Japanese gardens in the UK including:

Compton Acres Gardens (Dorset)

Holland Park (London)

Tatton Park Gardens (Cheshire)

Bonsai nurseries are also a source of inspiration

Chinese
960 – 1912

MARJORIE WILSON

The extreme length of this period is unusual, reflecting the Chinese respect for tradition and ancestry, which meant that artistic style and customs changed very little up to 1912. The artistic achievements of the Sung Dynasties (980–1127) are often likened to those of the Renaissance of Western Europe. There had been trade between China and the West since Roman times via the silk route through Byzantium but, although the West was attracted to Oriental goods and ideas, China remained virtually uninfluenced by Western ideas until after 1912.

In this vast country of many different climates and landscapes, agriculture was the main occupation and chief source of wealth. For centuries, the people were divided into seven grades – mandarins, warriors, scholars, bonzes, peasants, labourers and merchants.

The three major religious and philosophical influences were Confucius (the great teacher), Buddha (Buddhism spread from India and then to Japan) and Lao-Tse (Taoism). Each stressed the oneness of man with nature. Confucius emphasised the art of contemplation and taught that real enjoyment exists in simplicity. Buddhism taught the underlying principles of the preservation of life in all its forms and therefore using flowers sparingly.

Much of the symbolism relating to plant material has come from Taoism and a vast folklore of flowers has developed over the centuries.

China is frequently described as 'the flowery kingdom and the 'mother of gardens'. The Chinese garden was a retreat and place for contemplation. It was a small-scale replica of the natural landscape with water, rocks, trees and shrubs.

How and where flowers were used

The Chinese do not have a special alcove for flower arrangements as in Japan. Arrangements would have stood on low tables or stools; on tall stands a little under 1m high, on low chests or on the floor.

Flower and garden arts in China rank with paintings and music as cultural expression. Floral art is closely linked with furnishings, interior décor, painting and calligraphy, and harmony between them as a total composition is essential.

Pen-tsai (bonsai) dwarfing of trees for pot culture and *Pen-ching*, the creation of miniature landscapes in a tray or dish, date from the seventh century.

Typical settings

The Chinese practice is to prescribe the correct moment and surroundings for enjoying things. Chang T'su, a 12th-century Sung Dynasty writer gave 26 conditions for enjoying the Japanese apricot blossom and Yuan Hung-tao in his History of Vases gives 14 delightful conditions for enjoying flowers in general. They include: bright window; song of streams; wind among the pines; man of Chichow delivering wine; visiting monk understands brewing tea; Sung ink-stone; ancient bronze tripods; kettle sings deep in the night.

Symbolism

- The Taoist concept of the cosmos being composed of positive and negative forces gave rise to *Yin* and *Yang*:
  Yin (green) female, night, passiveness, winter, buds, water, earth, deep valleys, underside of leaves
  Yang (red) male, dragon, celestial, fire, action, rock, day, summer, open flowers, top surface of leaves

Yin and Yang

- All flowers because of their delicate beauty are feminine.
- Lan Ts'ai Ho, patron of florists, always carries a flower-filled basket.
- Birds formed part of the folklore symbolism and are often associated with plant material.

Overall characteristics of the period

Chinese philosophy sees man on equal terms with nature and not, as in the West, where man is the dominant element with nature as a background for his enjoyment. Therefore, as the author H. L. Li says, "when it is necessary to pick flowers and arrange them, it has to be done with humility and passion". There are no rules about arranging as in Japan, but floral art is generally based on the six canons of Hsieh, a fifth-century critic and painter. He stressed that all art must possess a living spirit of life force (*ch'i-yun*) over and above pure technique. Flower arrangements are restrained, with economy of material and regard for rhythm and space but they are never stylised.

- Arrangements are invariably asymmetrical. They emphasise irregularities and studied disorderliness.
- Flowers and branches are arranged in as naturalistic manner as possible.
- There may be one, two or, at most, three kinds of flowers in one vase. Baskets, however, are excepted from this and show massed flowers and colours.
- Flowers and branches should be in season and from the same environment or express a single symbolic idea.
- Flowers are not placed in pairs, symmetrical patterns or straight rows. Odd numbers are preferred.
- Interesting and well-shaped stems are selected, either trained in growth or manipulated after cutting.
- Flowers in one vase should be of one colour or, at most two or three harmonious colours. Strong contrasts, such as red and white, should not be used together. However, the colour of the vase should contrast with the flowers.
- Buds with open flowers break monotony.
- In a broad vase, plant material should be a few inches taller than the height of the vase. In a tall, slender vase, or a very small one, the plant material should be a few inches shorter than the vase.
- Accessories within an arrangement must be integrated into the design and be linked by the association of ideas. If several arrangements are used together, they must be of an equal height and the whole composition balanced.

Typical backgrounds

- characteristic upturned eaves of houses and pagodas
- columns of buildings painted in vermillion red, with carved flowers in blue and white
- enclosed courtyards with trees and plants in pots
- bamboo mats, rush matting and tiled floors
- lacquered furniture – terracotta red with black and gold decoration or black with gold
- dark furniture inlaid with mother-of-pearl

- carved and lacquered screens
- hanging wall scrolls of silk or paper with paintings or calligraphy
- naturalistic gardens with rocks and water

Interior scene depicted on an 18th century plate

Colour

Brightly coloured and showy flowers were preferred.

Yellow the Imperial colour, was used for the Emperor's robes, the tiles on the imperial palaces and, as it also stood for sanctity, was the colour of the Buddhist temple decorations.

Red the mandarin's colour stood for happiness, therefore, it was used for weddings and auspicious occasions.

White was the colour of mourning.

Green stood for eternal youth and everlasting qualities.

Containers

- The earliest containers were temple and ritual wine vessels of bronze in a variety of shapes. Later porcelain vases copied these shapes.
- *A Treatise of Vase Flowers* by Chang Ch' Ien-Te (1595) states that vases "should have a small mouth and thick base so that they will be steady and not lose vapours". Bronze vases were chosen for winter and spring arrangements and porcelain for summer and autumn. Vase shapes had attractive names, such as 'one twig', 'paper-beater', 'gall', 'goose-necked', 'beaker' and 'gourd shaped'.

Porcelain examples were usually intricately patterned, though celadon, in a range of subtle green colours, was more usually plain. Enamel and cloisonné enamel, in which colours are kept apart by thin outline plates, were also used.

Typical vase forms used as containers and a bamboo basket (bottom row, right)

- Baskets took many attractive and varied shapes, including two-handled ones. China was the first country to make baskets specifically for flowers. Hanging baskets, sometimes shown being carried on a hoe, were highly favoured containers.

Hanging baskets, sometimes shown as being carried on a hoe, were particularly popular as containers

- Originally, every vase was designed with its own base or stand, usually of carved wood. Some stands were elaborate and were virtually pedestals.

Mechanics

Probably no more than forked crossed twigs wedged in the neck vase, similar to the Japanese *kubari*.

Vase bases were specially designed for each vase

Suggested accessories

Of all the styles and periods, the Chinese shows most strongly the grouping of arrangement(s) with accessories as a studied composition, both for symbolic and artistic effect. The following are frequently seen in paintings or silk embroideries:

- drum or decorated bin of scrolls
- brush pot with paintings and calligraphy brushes
- incense burners
- lacquered stools and boxes
- jade pieces in many colours
- ivories
- decorated porcelain plates
- fly swat with tassel
- carved figurines
- books
- hanging wall scrolls

Other accessories, which would suggest China are elaborate paper kites, fans, paper lanterns, Fo dogs, table rocks and bowls of auspicious fruit.

Typical Winter arrangement of *Prunus persica* branches and camellia. Accessories include a lacquer bin of scrolls, incense burner and bowl with pomegranate. Drawing based on a 17th century print by Ting Liang-hsien.

References and resources

Plant material

The most important and frequently used are listed first with their symbolic meaning in English:

Anemone sp., death
Bamboo sp., flexibility and strength
Chrysanthemum sp., autumn, long-life; linked with the wild goose.
Citrus medica, health, wealth, blessing, happiness
Cymbidium sp., spring, karma, seclusion, friendship
Gramineae, humility
Iris sp., manhood
Magnolia denudata, *M. liliflora*, affluence, power
Narcissus tazetta orientalis, New Year, purity
Nelumbo nucifera, summer, Buddha's secret flower, nobility, purity; linked with mandarin duck, in pairs for marital bliss and the egret for purity
Orchis sp., nobility
Paeonia suffruticosa, king of flowers, spring, rank, power, beauty, good fortune – linked with peacock and pheasant
Phyllostachys, fidelity, humility
Pinus sp., bamboo sp. and *Prunus* sp. blossom were the 'Three Friends of the Cold Season'
Pinus tabuliformis, most revered of trees, nobility, majesty, wisdom, longevity; linked with the crane
Prunus domestica, winter, friendship and brotherliness when with peach blossom
Prunus mume, winter, good fortune, perseverance; it is linked with the magpie
Prunus persica blossom, youthful beauty
Prunus persica fruit, longevity
Prunus sp., delicate beauty of women
Punica granatum, fertility
Salix sp., gracefulness, devotion, mercy; linked with the swallow.

Other frequently used plant materials:

Acorus calamus
Althaea rosea
Artemisia sp.
Camellia sinensis
Catalpa sp.
Chaenomeles sp.
Daphne sp.
Hemerocallis sp.
Hibiscus sp.
Hosta plantaginea
Jasminum sp.
Juniperus sp.
Lagenaria vulgaris
Lilium lancifolium
Nandina domestica
Nerium oleander
Osmanthus sp.
Rosa banksiae
Rosa chinensis
Rosa hugonis
Rosa rugosa
Salix sp.
Symphyotrichum
Syringa sp.
Viburnum farreri
Wisteria sinensis

Places to see

Museums and galleries

Since the 17th century, chinoiserie has been popular in Europe and in this country so there are examples of Chinese porcelain in many art galleries, museums and stately homes. Some Chippendale furniture shows Chinese decoration.

V&A Museum (London)

Historic buildings and monuments

National Trust properties for Chinese wallpaper

Royal Pavilion, Brighton (East Sussex) for Chinese decoration

Places

Chinatown (London)

Gardens

Royal Botanic Gardens, Kew (London) for the Chinese pagoda

Italian Renaissance
1400–1600

PAOLO BURGER AND INNA DUFOUR

The Renaissance was the European revival based on classical concepts after the fear, dangers and plagues of the Middle or Dark Ages. The Early Renaissance is usually dated from 1300 when such a rebirth began gaining ground in Italy. The High Renaissance was from 1500 to 1600.

It was caused by various factors including changed political and social conditions, powerful ruling families who patronised the arts, urban development, easier travel, widespread commerce and exchange of visits with the East. This prosperity was felt all over Europe.

In Italy, first in Florence with the Medici family and later in Urbino with the Montefeltrea family, and in Mantova with the Gonzagas, all the arts prospered, giving rise to one of the most important cultural developments in history.

With the invention of printing many publishing houses were founded enabling the classics to become more widely known. Until this time Art had mainly been for the glorification of God, but now 'Man' himself became an important influence.

How and where flowers were used

In Dante we find the earliest reference to the use of cut flowers:

"Quand'ella ha in testa una ghirlanda d'erba ...."
(When she has a garland of flowers on her head ....).

Petrarch, Boccaccio and other writers confirm this use. The garland was certainly the decoration most used by Florentine ladies in reviving Greek and Roman traditions. Later, to show off their riches, these garlands were made of gold and precious stones by the Florentine goldsmiths. One of those in greatest demand was the father of Ghirlandaio, the painter. From this artist we have the best evidence of the use of cut flowers as well as the life-style and important people of his age.

Great use was made of cut flowers and herbs, especially in Florence, during processions and feast days like *Calendimaggio*, on 1 May.

Gradually, flowers lost the meaning of humble homage to God and became more and more secular decoration. For example, strewn flowers and fruits, *Prunus avium, Rosa* sp., and *Cytisus* sp., are seen on white linen tablecloths at rich banquets.

Garlands and festoons in designs taken from classical origins, grew more lavish and ornate in Renaissance times, especially in northern Italy, with painters like Crivelli, Mantegna, Schiavone and Tura. New decorative elements were often those imported from distant countries – corals, crystals and exotic fruits.

In a number of paintings and also in literature references, we find cultivated pot-flowers – flowering plants, herbs, or topiary evergreens in terracotta, majolica or marble urns or pots. Such pots were placed almost anywhere – in windows, against walls, on parapets and on the steps of houses. This habit is still common today all over Italy.

Typical settings

- wide bright spaces and light through full, rounded arches
- architectural features inspired by Greek and Roman styles
- windows and doorways surmounted by pediments; loggias designed to frame green landscapes
- white surfaces framed by grey stone; red brick framed by light marble
- palaces and villas finished with hewn *bugnato* or smooth *conci* stone
- symmetry and harmony triumph
- floors in coloured marble or terracotta tiles enriched with smaller, coloured ones
- walls in plain plaster; only occasionally was intarsia, inlaid wood mosaic, panelling used for rooms in rich palaces
- ceilings, often frescoed or covered in carved wooden recessed squares
- fireplaces framed in marble, stone or plaster with richly decorated fire dogs forming an integral part of the room's architecture

Detail of flowers from 15th century painting, San Marco Museum, Florence

Panel in Urbino Palace

Fittings and textiles

Furniture of the early Renaissance was simply designed, often decorated with gilt gesso. In the 16th century it became fashionable to have carved wood furniture which was neither painted nor gilded. Typical examples are seen in some paintings of the period – richly carved chests and commodes and walnut wardrobes with intarsia decoration. But even in wealthy homes furniture was sparse by present day standards.

Fabrics Persian damasks, Genoese velvets and silk brocades were often embroidered with gold thread and encrusted with precious stones.

Carpets used in Italy during the Renaissance were oriental. The artists Giotto, Mantegna, Ghirlandaio and Carpaccio all painted Caucasian and Anatolian rugs, as did Holbein the Younger.

The development of gardens

Italian Renaissance gardens were new in style, inspired by classical ideals of order and beauty, and intended for the pleasure of the view and the landscape beyond, for contemplation, and for the enjoyment of the sights, sounds and smells of the garden itself.

They were planned to be an integral part of the architecture of a building. Even plants and trees were pruned and trimmed to give them shapes which were part of the architectural scheme, and borders and beds were geometrical in shape. Advantage was taken, for the first time, of natural landscape contours and ingenious hydraulic engineering provided jets, sprinkling fountains, waterfalls and even sound effects. The most famous example is at the Villa d'Este at Tivoli.

Topiary ornaments were part of the architectural scheme of some gardens

Gardens sometimes contained graceful features such as pergolas, arbours and aviaries

Symbolism

The religious symbolism of the Middle Ages continued, and flowers placed in churches or shown in altarpieces contained messages for the populace who could not read. For example, *Lilium candidum* stood for purity and chastity. Other flower symbolism included:

- *Convallaria majalis*, purity
- *Iris* sp., majesty, Mary Queen of Heaven
- *Rosa gallica* love, the Virgin's sorrow
- *Rosa alba* the Virgin's gladness
- *Dianthus plumarius*, human love, or in the Virgin's hand, divine love
- 7 *Aquilegia*, seven gifts of the Holy Spirit
- *Bellis perennis*, innocence
- *Viola odorata*, humility, sorrow
- *Viola* sp. or *Trifolium* sp., the Trinity
- sheaf of *Triticum* sp., bread broken at the Eucharist
- *Lilium rubrum*, blood of the passion

Roses in flat woven basket from an altar piece by Beato Angelico – Perugia – 1437

Symbolic use of *Aquilegia* and *Dianthus* in a glass tumbler from a Van der Goes altar piece

Often on the heads of children, angels and cherubs, **garlands** generally signified youthfulness and friendship, but had special meanings according to the use of fruit, flowers and leaves:

- *Laurus* sp., glory.
- *Lilium* or *Rosa* sp., beauty.
- *Papaver* sp., night, sleep.
- *Punica granatum*, goodwill, fertility.

Containers

- Crockery and decorative containers were made in Florence (Montelupe), Orvieto and Faenza. The latter produced the best majolica ware.

- Jugs, dishes, bowls and apothecaries' jars were decorated with stylized floral designs sometimes containing coats of arms, portraits and mythological scenes. Main colours were: green, brown, dark blue, yellow ochre and black.

- Rough terracotta pottery was commonly used by poor and rich.

- Venice, or rather the island of Murano, was the main centre of glass manufacture. After the 16th century, when production reached its height in both design and embellishment, painted decoration ceased. This may be attributed to two factors: the discovery of crystal glass and the influence of the style from Tuscany, where importance was placed on shape and style rather than on applied decoration.

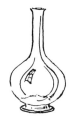

Decanter shaped glass vase – 1572

- In paintings silver utensils, tureens, trays, dishes and wine jugs or ewers are often shown displayed at banquets and feasts.

Majolica ware from Tuscany – 15th century

References and resources

Plant material

During the 15th and 16th centuries, an increasing interest in the sciences led to great interest in botanical drawing and painting. For example, Botticelli's *La Primavera* contains more than 40 different species of flowers cultivated and studied by his humanist and scientist friends.

Many new plants were imported from the Middle East and cultivated in the gardens of the large villas and palaces. Generally speaking, however, the flowers and foliage shown in paintings are those typical of Mediterranean vegetation.

Detail from La Primavera – Botticelli

Flowers
Aquilegia vulgaris
Anemone sp.
Bellis perennis
Calendula sp.
Campanula rotundifolia
Carlina sp.
Centaurea cyanus
Convallaria majalis
Convolvulus sp.
Crataegus monogyna
Cyclamen sp.
Cnicus sp.
Cytisus sp.
Dianthus caryophyllus
Dianthus plumarius
Digitalis purpurea
Echinops sp.
Genista
Helleborus sp.
Hyacinthus sp.
Iris sp.
Jasminum sp.
Lavandula spica
Lilium sp.
Lilium candidum
Lonicera sp.
Lychnis sp.
Muscari sp.
Myosotis sp.
Narcissus sp.
Onopordon sp.
Papaver sp.
Primula x *pubescens*
Ranunculus sp.
Rosa (double pink)
Rosa alba
Rosa gallica
Spartium sp.
Taraxacum officinale
Veronica sp.
Vinca sp.
Viola sp.

Foliage
Acanthus mollis
Arbutus sp.
Arum italicum
Buxus sp.
Cupressus sp.
Fagus sylvatica
Hedera sp.
Ilex sp.
Laurus nobilis
Myrtus communis
Nerium oleander
Olea europaea
Phoenix dactylifera
Pinus sp.
Populus sp.
Quercus sp.
Ruta graveolens
Vitis sp.

Edible fruits and vegetables
almond
apple
artichoke
cherry
chestnut
citron
cucumber
fig
grape
hazelnut
lemon
melon
olive
orange
peach
pear
plum
pomegranate
quince
wheat

Herbs
Borago officinalis
Chamaemelum nobile syn. *Anthemis nobilis*
Ocimum basilicum
Origanum vulgare
Salvia officinalis
Salvia rosmarinus
Thymus sp.

New plants during this period included:
Amaranthus sp.
Cactaceae
Canna sp.
Fritillaria imperialis
Paeonia sp.
Syringa x *persica*
Tulipa sp.

Places to see

Museums and galleries

Borghese Gallery & Museum, Rome (Italy)

Hampton Court (Surrey) in the Mantegna Gallery, Andrea Mantegna's drawings *The Triumphs of Caesar*. Also, the garden and the labyrinth.

National Gallery (London) paintings by the Italian School, but especially Carlo Crivelli's *Annunciation with Saint Emidius*, *Virgin and Child with Saints Francis and Sebastian* and *The Immaculate Conception*; Andrea Mantegna's *The Vestal Virgin Tuccia with a Sieve*, *A Woman Drinking*, *The Agony in the Garden*; Fra Filippo Lippi's *The Annunciation*; Antonello da Messina's *Saint Jerome in his Study*; Piero della Francesca's *The Baptism of Christ*; Cosimo Tura's *The Virgin and Child Enthroned* and *A Muse (Calliope)*; Bramantino's *The Adoration of Kings*; the works of Botticelli, Fra Angelico, Bergognone and others.

Uffizi Gallery, Florence (Italy)

V&A Museum (London) Florentine furniture, Della Robbia ceramics and Raphael's tapestry cartoons.

Della Robbia ceramic panel in white, blue, green and lemon

Tudor

1485–1603

DAPHNE VAGG

An era of comparative peace followed the Wars of the Roses. There was no longer need to fortify castles, so manor houses were being built instead with space for pleasure gardens.

Renaissance ideas spread northwards from Italy with new interest in learning and the arts.

There was exploration and discovery in science, horticulture and in lands overseas.

Trade expanded with Mediterranean countries and further east. A new and powerful middle class of politicians and merchants was emerging.

How and where flowers were used

In the house, there was little occasional furniture, so flowers stood on the floor and window sills or hearths in summer. Evidence for the use of flowers in the home is found in writing and paintings of the time. The herbalist and gardener John Parkinson wrote ".... fresh bowls in every corner and flowers tied upon them and sweet briar, stock, gilly-flowers, pinks, wallflowers and other sweet flowers in glasses and pots in every window and chimney", while John Gerard, another herbalist and botanist said: "... daffodils ... are so exceeding sweete that very few are sufficient to perfume a whole chamber". Holbein's paintings of Sir Thomas More and family, and of George Gisze, a merchant, show the use of flowers in vases.

At weddings

Salvia rosmarinus and *Cytisus,* often gilded, were worn on sleeves and hats, or carried before the bride in a cup tied with bridelaces (gaily coloured ribbons).

Wedding flowers from 'A Fête at Bermondsey' – Joris Hoefnagel

Sweet William from Gerard's Herball

From Holbein's portrait of George Gisze

At funerals

Sprigs of *Salvia rosmarinus* were thrown into graves and Robert Herrick wrote: "Grow for two ends, it matters not at all Be't for my bridall, or my burial."

On special occasions

- Flowers and herbs were strewn on the ground as in medieval times.
- Crown garlands were worn on the head at banquets, and by priests at special church festivals.
- Morris dancers, popular in the period, wore flower-garlanded hats.

Typical settings

- timbered and plastered walls
- linenfold panelling in oak
- rush-strewn floors mixed with herbs and sweet flowers
- diamond-patterned casement windows
- Turkish and oriental carpets on tables, not floors
- tapestries and embroideries almost always with floral motifs
- knot gardens and topiary
- wood – mainly oak, some elm and other native woods
- painted plasterwork, panelling and furniture
  "... it would not be very wrong to say that 16th century interior decoration abhorred an unpainted surface ...... and covered whatever it could reach in bright and simple colours" – from *Connoisseur Period Guides, Tudor 1500–1603*.

Elizabethan embroidery on a hood (V&A Museum)

Two knots from Lawson's Country Housewife's Garden

(left) The Tre-Foy
(right) Oval

Typical fittings and textiles

- velvet, brocade and worsted
- leather and fur
- Peasants wore fustian, a dark dyed cotton twill, and russet, a coarse homespun reddish-brown or grey cloth

Symbolism

The religious symbolism of flowers in Renaissance Italy seems not to have been used by the Tudors. A glass plaque at Loseley House (see page 68) however, portrays royal fleur-de-lys with the roses of York and Lancaster to symbolize the ancestry and majesty of Queen Elizabeth I. Many portraits show the sitter holding one flower. For example, in the National Portrait Gallery, Henry VII and Edward VI are both portrayed holding the Tudor rose; Elizabeth of York, the white rose; Katherine of Aragon, green wheat ears and Margaret Pole, Countess of Salisbury, honeysuckle. Apart from this, the Tudors believed that flowers and herbs actually warded off disease and pestilence and were protection against the plague. Sweet and spicy scents were also helpful in abating the unpleasant smells of unwashed bodies and sewer-like streets.

Overall characteristics of the period

Simple, uncontrived bunches with quite a lot of foliage. Flowers have the look of being arranged in the hand, then placed in the container. There were probably no mechanics, the neck of the container holding the flowers in place. The style is somewhere between the restrained Italian Renaissance use of flowers and the exuberance of the Dutch flowerpiece. The emphasis was always on scent to "attemper the aire, coole and make fresh the place to the delight and comfort of such as are therein" – John Gerard.

Colour

Houses were painted brilliant colours on indoor walls and ceilings – red, blue, green, gold and silver.

On the outside of houses between the timbering, plaster was painted in minium (burnt orange), cinnabar (brown red), rose madder (purple pink) and orpiment (yellow) rather than the white we customarily see nowadays.

Imported embroidery silks were to be had in such colours as crimson, watchet blue, ash, marigold, tawny, dove-coloured, lady-blush, green, pound citron and brazil – from *the Letters of John Johnson, Cloth Merchant 1542-52*.

Flower arrangements were polychromatic in bright mixed colours.

Containers

pewter tankards, goblets and jugs.

glass plain simple decanter shapes, goblets.

Also, coconut cups; treen platters and bowls; clay mugs and bowls, simple in shape, thick and unglazed on the outside; blue and white imported Delft-style pottery; leather tankards and bottles.

Suggested accessories

No accessories appear to have been used as such at the time but, for period atmosphere the following might be suitable:

Potpourri in bowls a long-lasting mixture of dried petals (especially rose) herbs and spices.

Pomanders oranges stuck all over with cloves and tied with ribbons. Sometimes they were metal, pierced holders for herbs and spices, carried over the wrist, in the hand or hanging down from the waist.

Tussie-mussie or nosegay a small simple bunch of flowers and herbs held in the hand.

Also, rush-nip lights, beeswax candles, painted miniatures, a lute and bridelaces (silk or buckram ribbons).

A tussie-mussie from a painting of Charles Brandon, Duke of Suffolk

Flowers in the hand from a portrait of Anne of Cleves

References and resources

Plant material

Flowers
Shakespeare alone refers to more than 100 plant forms in his plays. And, with the exception of *Chrysanthemum, Dahlia, Gladiolus* and flowering shrubs not native to this country, the Tudors knew most of the flowers we have today. They were smaller than our modern hybrids. Native wildflowers were brought into cultivation, and many others had already been introduced. Most important was the gillyflower, a name used for clove-scented flowers of the *Dianthus* family, Caryophyllaceae, such as *D. barbatus*, *D. caryophyllus* and *D. plumarius*.

Popular also were:

Aquilegia vulgaris
Auricula sp.,
Centaurea cyanus
Digitalis purpurea
Dipsacus sylvestris
Galium odoratum
Helleborus sp.
Lonicera sp.
Narcissus sp.
Primula veris
Primula vulgaris (especially the Hose-in-Hose and Jack-in-the-Green types)
Tanacetum vulgare
Viola sp.

And, of course the *Rosa* and *Lilium* species, *Iris pseudacorus* (fleur-de-lys) and *Tulipa* sp.

Foliage
All kinds of herbs and sweet-smelling leaves, but especially:

Lavandula spica
Mentha sp.
Origanum majorana
Ruta graveolens
Salvia sp. including *Salvia rosmarinus*
Santolina chamaecyparissus
Thymus sp.

Also, species of:

Buxus
Hedera
Ilex
Juniperus
Laurus
Myrtus
Taxus

> "Get ivy and Hull (holly) woman, deck up thy house."
> *Thomas Tusser (1573)*

> "Altho we do trimme up our parlours with greene boughs, freshe herbs and vine leaves, no nation does it more trimmely, nor more sightly than they doe in England."
> *Levinus Lemnius (1560)*

Places to see

Historic buildings and monuments

Hampton Court Palace (London)

Hardwick Hall (Derbyshire)

Levens Hall (Cumbria)

Littlecote House (Wiltshire)

Little Moreton Hall (Cheshire)

Shakespeare Birthplace Trust properties (Warwickshire)

Pictures for inspiration

(see also section on Symbolism)

Family of Sir Thomas More. after Holbein. The version at Nostell Priory, Yorkshire, shows three flower arrangements at the back of the room. The National Portrait Gallery version shows only two as later descendants of the family have been painted in on the right.

Portait of the Merchant George Gisze (1497–1562), Holbein (Staatliche Museum, Berlin). Amid the paraphernalia of a merchant's office a simple arrangement of *Dianthus caryophyllus, Salvia rosmarinus* and possibly *Galium odoratum* stands in a glass vase on the desk.

A Fete at Bermondsey, Joris Hoefnagel (Hatfield House, Hertfordshire). Guests are celebrating a wedding and a man carries a bride-cup and possibly yellow roses decorated with bridelaces.

Glass plaque (Loseley House, Surrey), see details under **Symbolism**.

Glass plaque at Loseley House

Portrait of Charles Brandon, Duke of Suffolk c. 1540-1545 – in National Portrait Gallery, artist unknown. He holds a tussie-mussie of herbs and flowers, including *Viola* sp. and possibly *Armeria maritima.*

People to look up

Artists

Hans Eworth (worked in London c.1545-1574)

Nicholas Hilliard (1547-1619) – miniaturist

Hans Holbein (1497-1543)

Isaac Oliver (*d.* 1617) – miniaturist

Herbalists

John Gerard published his famous *The Herball* in 1597

Henry Lyte's *Niewe Herball,* 1578

William Turner, who is known as the father of English botany, wrote *A New Herball,* 1551

Writers

Francis Bacon's essay *Of Gardens* (1597)

Edmund Spenser's poems and William Shakespeare's plays contain many references to plants and flowers

Thomas Tusser (*c.*1515-1580) wrote a long rhyming treatise on gardening in 1557, later enlarged to become *Five Hundred Points of Good Husbandry*

Dutch and Flemish
1600–1800

JOAN WEATHERLAKE

In a manner similar to that of Tudor England, 17th-century Holland enjoyed a rapid rise to the status of great European power. Its trade and colonization spread to all parts of the world.

Society at home was dominated by rich, middle class merchants whose prosperity came from agriculture, fishing, cloth from Leiden, ceramics from Delft, linen from Haarlem, velvet from Utrecht and precious metals from Amsterdam.

Cultural life was intensified and new universities flourished, poetry reached new heights and painting especially became the foremost expression of the national culture. Apart from the quality of the Dutch 17th-century paintings, the enormous quantity produced in a small country in such a short space of time was quite remarkable. Interest in horticulture was widespread.

At the same time, the north had firmly adopted Protestantism with its strict morals and concern with the inevitability of death. It became fashionable to brighten rooms in the dark and gloomy Dutch interiors with vivid floral paintings rather than with vases of real flowers.

Even the less-than-rich purchased paintings as an investment, perhaps because the shortage of land in the country made property investment difficult. It also tied in with their love of gardens and plants, which could then be enjoyed during the long, cold winters.

How and where flowers were used

In flower-pieces usually as arrangements in containers with one or two flowers lying at the base. Less often, notably in paintings by the artist Jan Davidsz de Heem, flowers and fruit festoon a portrait, or are used as a wall swag.

In general use simpler arrangements stood on windowsills and sometimes on the floor or mantelpiece. Paintings of the grand banquet piece also show flowers standing on the meal table.

After de Heem
Swag of flowers and fruit, tied with ribbon and suspended from a ring

Typical settings

- buildings, predominantly brick with stone facings to doorways and windows
- stepped gabled roofs
- black and white chequered floors
- uncluttered interiors with a few pieces of solidly made, simply designed furniture
- shuttered windows with small rectangular leaded windowsills and panes
- oriental carpets as table coverings
- hangings of velvet, silk or linen, sometimes fringed, falling in graceful folds, often from rings on a curtain pole
- heavy, but well-proportioned pewter utensils, candlesticks, etc.
- fireplaces decorated with Delft tiles, and heavy wooden mantelpieces
- velvet upholstered chairs with brass studding
- tables set with pewter, gleaming glass and white drapery, sometimes lace-edged and often showing the square fold lines of the linen press

Detail from Jan Steen's 'The Burgher of Delft and his daughter'

Symbolism

The melancholy and strictly moral influence of the Calvinist reformers meant that man must be continually reminded of the transience of life and of the sins of vanity and indulging in the pleasures of the senses. This theme, known as *Vanitas* from the Latin word for vanity, is found in almost all Dutch still-life painting.

Objects shown symbolized the following:

- **earthly existence** books, paper scrolls, jewellery, deeds, scientific instruments, purses, musical instruments, shells, objets d'art, weapons, pipes, dice, playing cards, goblets
- **transience of life** flowers especially *Anemone* and *Rosa* sp., marred and peeled fruit, holes in leaves, insects and reptiles which destroyed flowers and fruit, skulls, watches, clocks, hour-glasses, candlesticks with lighted candles
- **resurrection** ears of corn, *Hedera*, sprigs of laurel, bird's nest with eggs, butterflies (symbolic of the soul)

Another form of symbolism was seen through the hierarchy of flowers. In the early period, the flowers depicting the Holy Family e.g., *Fritillaria imperialis*, *Iris* sp. and *Lilium* sp., were placed at the top of the arrangement. Jan Brueghel also painted the 'noble' flowers *Dianthus caryophyllus*, *Rosa* sp. and *Paeonia* sp. with the humble wildflowers at the bottom.

Overall characteristics of the period

In this period there are two quite different types of flower arrangements recorded by the artists:

The Dutch flower piece which was one of the many forms of still life painting popular at the time. There was also the fruit piece, fish piece, game piece etc.

The flower piece was often painted for rich merchant patrons to show off the plants recently acquired for their gardens or simply to demonstrate the artist's technical ability to observe and reproduce the qualities of light, texture and botanical detail. Flowers of many seasons appear together, taken from notebook drawings. The design would not have existed as an actual arrangement.

The flower arrangement that appears as a less important part of an interior, portrait or banquet-piece.

The style of the flower paintings changed over the 200 year period and may be roughly divided as follows:

c1600 – 1650 The influence of the Italian Renaissance was strong. Arrangements are stiff, compact and naive, with little depth and few flowers used as a rule. The shape is oval with accessories placed at the base – perhaps a shell, flower or insect. Examples: Jan Brueghel, Ambrosius Bosschaert (Elder and Younger), Roeland Savery.

After Ambrosius Bosschaert the Younger – 1635

c1650 – 1700 Arrangements became looser with more space, movement and depth created by turning flowers to show the sides and back. Graceful downward flowing lines are featured and more accessories are shown at the base. Examples: Jacob van Walscapelle, Willem van Aelst, Jan Davidsz de Heem, Rachel Ruysch.

c1700 – 1800 The style became more exuberant and sweeping. Large full-blown flowers and heavy fruit are found quite high in the design. Hogarth curves run through the composition with different groupings of accessories at the base. Examples: Paul Thedorus van Brussel, Jan van Huysum, Jan van Os.

After Willem van Aelst – 1663

Particular characteristics of the period

- massed flowers of many different varieties, but not packed tightly and space is used; flowers of all seasons appear together
- overall shape is round, oval or square
- large and important flowers at the top
- turning of flowers to show back and sides creates depth
- rich, glowing polychromatic colours, also white and pale tints
- sweeping S-line seen in later arrangements
- the vanitas theme shown in accessories, broken stems, holed leaves and marred fruit
- little added foliage

In *Period Flower Arrangement* (Barrows, 1952), the author Margaret Marcus says of the 17th century:

> "The mood of the baroque is dynamic and boldly confident. Such lush abundance has never been seen before, or since, in Western art… The important thing is to create a consistent asymmetrical movement from right to left, or vice versa. There must be no quiet spot but an exciting movement of arching stems, nodding flowers and curling petals. The final effect should be neither rigid nor bunched but voluptuous and graceful."

Typical backgrounds

Early paintings show a simple, plain, often dark background, or a wall niche with curved top, or an arched window opening through which a landscape in the style of the Italian Renaissance painters is visible. In the middle and later part of the period, backgrounds are usually dark, but the artists Paul Theodorus van Brussel, Jan van Os and Jan van Huysum also used a brownish green with the faintest suggestion of trees and a garden.

Bases are invariably of marble or stone, grey or brown in colour. Later in the period, shaping suggests the end of a balustrade or shelf. On tables, containers of flowers or fruit stand directly on the cloth.

Colour

Flower arrangements are all richly polychromatic but paintings show the room interiors to be cool, greyed colours. Black and white were much used in costumes. Draperies and cloths are often in chestnut brown and many shades of green, especially a dull olive.

Containers

All containers are sturdy – even the glass is thick and practical.

Early period clear glass decanter shapes, brown glazed pots, Delftware, often bulbous with a narrow neck

Middle period glass, including Venetian, knobbed tumbler-shaped vases, metal urns and Delftware

Late period squat terracotta and metal urns, low woven baskets appear in all periods almost invariably as shown here

Glass decanter   Metal urn   Knobbed tumbler

Flowers in a basket with berries and insects

Suggested accessories

Accessories grouped at the base of the container and insects, caterpillars and butterflies within the arrangement are typical of Dutch/Flemish paintings and not seen elsewhere. The vanitas theme accounts for this but it is probable also that artists delighted in portraying the change in colour, form and texture and the minute detail. Such weight at the bottom of the picture was also needed to balance the large open flowers or fruit at the top.

The vanitas accessories in flower pieces include:

- birds, bird's nest with eggs (often blue), bird's feathers
- moths, butterflies, dragonflies, insects
- watch (with blue ribbon) hour-glass, skull
- shells, snails, caterpillars and lizards

Table accessories include:

- candlesticks
- Delftware
- gilt standing salts
- glass and metal goblets
- jugs and ewers
- knives
- knobbed glasses
- nautilus cups
- pewter utensils
- tilted plates and jugs

Typical vanitas accessories in still life and flower paintings

The observer is reminded of the vanity of worldly things, the brevity of life and the frailty of man

References and resources

Plant material

Flowers

Tulipa sp. – striped, streaked and parrot types especially. 'Tulipomania' swept Holland in the first part of the 17th century with fortunes changing hands for special bulbs. The colour breaks (a virus) were not understood and much time and money were spent trying to propagate them.

Also portrayed by artists:

Althaea rosea
Aquilegia sp.
Anemone sp.
Auricula sp.
Calendula sp.
Centaurea cyanus
Convallaria majalis
Dianthus caryophyllus
Fritillaria sp. including *F. imperialis*
Hyacinthus sp.
Ipomoea sp.
Iris sp.
Jasminum sp.
Lilium sp. including *L. candidum, L. martagon*
Narcissus sp.
Paeonia sp.
Papaver sp.
Rosa sp.
Syringa vulgaris
Tropaeolum major
Viburnum opulus 'Roseum' and *Viola*.

Foliage

Leaves other than those on flower stalks were seldom used. Those portrayed include species of *Rosa, Papaver, Paeonia, Iris, Tropaeolum* and *Vitis*.

Edible fruits

Luscious fruit was shown in Delftware bowls, baskets and on pewter plates. The half-peeled lemon with peel curling over the edge of the table appears in countless paintings. Other fruits seen are:

apricots
cherries
ears of corn and barley
grapes with vine leaves
melons
nuts (including chestnuts in outer prickly cases, hazelnuts and walnuts)
oranges
peaches
pineapples
plums
pomegranates
warted gourds

Places to see

Flower paintings

Ashmolean Museum (Oxford)

The Fitzwilliam Museum (Cambridge)

National Gallery (London) for paintings by Anthony van Dyck (1599-1641), Peter Paul Rubens (1577-1640), Rembrandt van Rijn (1606-69), Jacob van Ruisdael (1628-82) and Aelbert Cuyp (1620-91) for landscapes. See also Johannes Vermeer (1632-75), Pieter de Hooch (1629-84) and Gerard ter Borch (1617-81) for interiors and scenes of everyday life.

Dutch-style gardens

These are flat, level gardens and feature water, parterres, statues and topiary. The Dutch style was more intimate than the grander French style.

Lyme Park (Cheshire)

Queen's Garden, Royal Botanic Gardens, Kew (London)

American Colonial

1620–1800

JEAN TAYLOR

This period is a lesson to us in husbandry. It began the now worldwide interest in drying and preserving flowers and leaves. Plants were an inseparable part of everyday living, so there was considerable interest in cultivation and new introductions. It was a time for great botanists, collectors and naturalists and for a huge interchange of plants between the old and new worlds.

It was a time of one of the greatest exoduses from one country to another. First the Pilgrims, and later the Puritans, left Britain. The Puritans, eager to carry the gospel and to escape from religious intolerance, were joined by people with varied motives such as a desire for riches, to escape from an unpleasant life, or pure adventure.

Life was not decorative or indulgent, but was purposeful and without any frills. Whole families emigrated together making arduous voyages on ships barely 17m long with their servants and all their possessions, including, animals, implements, seeds, roots, saplings and household possessions, even nails. They were brave, able, determined people, skilled in the art of wasting nothing and making do.

Early 17th-century living was difficult in the extreme: the first few years were a continuing struggle to overcome illness and hunger, hostilities with indigenous tribes and the wild land. In the winter of 1609-10, the main settlement in Virginia lost 440 of its 500 inhabitants.

Then the settlers began to master frontier living and the colonies grew and became strong. Although the first half of the 17th century was one of great hardship, the latter half and the 18th century were years of growth, stability, comfort and elegance, with leisure time, craftsmen supplying needs and ships carrying more and more elegant furniture and china from Europe.

American colonial home

AMERICAN COLONIAL 79

Flower arrangements in the manner of Colonial America should typify either the early days of hardship or the later years of more elegant living. There is a marked contrast between them.

Flowers in a glass vase from a portrait of Elizabeth Wensley (c 1670)

Four-tiered Bristol-made Delft vase with snippets of *Anthriscus sylvestris*, *Calendula*, *Tanacetum vulgare*, *Nigella*, *Celosia cristata*, *Mentha*, *Amaranthus*, *Chrysanthemum parthenium* and *C. frutescens*

How and where flowers were used

17th century

In the early 1600s, there was no time for flower decoration but utensils holding fresh flowers, and bunches of flowers and leaves hanging to dry would be seen in the stillroom. They awaited processing into spirits, syrups, salves, plasters, waters, pills, and powders. Plants were used for medicines, flavourings, narcotics, insect repellents, perfumes, dyes, painkillers, drinks, potpourri, tonics, cosmetics and for smoking. They were, therefore, an essential and integral part of everyday living and the housewife had to be skilled in the arts of distilling, fermenting, drying and preserving, in addition to a knowledge of cookery and gardening. Stewing herbs were used on the floors to ward off disease.

18th century

Nosegays were particularly valued for changing the air in a room. Decorative arrangements of fresh or dried flowers were used in rooms and placed on tables and other furniture.

Typical settings and backgrounds

Early colonial home life centred around a dominating alcove containing several fireplaces with different temperatures for cooking. The keeping room was the family living and dining room. The stillroom, either a little space in the kitchen or a separate, coolhouse, was the place for making cheeses, starting wines, brewing beers, setting dyes, making plasters, salves, oils and waters from plants, and drying leaves and flowers. Sparse, handmade furniture at first was followed by elegant, imported, comfortable furniture after 1700.

Bouquet of flowers in a glass vase

17th century

- simple wigwams
- wattle and daub walls; packed earth floors, rush strewn
- half-timbered interiors
- sturdy front doors with long strap hinges and wooden bars for security
- animal skin floor coverings
- rush-thatched roofs, often native palmetto
- hand-hewn beams of wooden framework, left exposed
- windows of imported glass, small panes set in lead strips, but only shutters at first

Half-timbered interior with a Windsor chair

18th century

- substantially-built houses based on English medieval models, sometimes of brick
- painted interiors, pine panelling, cedar-grained panels and marble and wood-grained surfaces
- alcoves set in walls
- Windsor chairs
- Queen Anne style furniture, also Chippendale
- Hepplewhite and Sheraton influence, with inlays and veneers replacing earlier carved surfaces
- tray-top tea tables in cherry wood
- red painted, slipper foot highboys

A table with six legs designed by George Hepplewhite in the 18th century

Overall characteristics of the period

At first there were probably small informal bunches or posies of fresh or dried in mixed colours and varieties. In the 18th century, there were rounded, massed bouquet-style dried flowers and at Colonial Williamsburg Historic Area, present-day arrangers working in period style have also used fan-shaped arrangements.

Colour

17th century

- bright colours of fresh flowers
- subtle colours of home-dyed fabrics with dyes made from plants
- natural wood colours
- colour choice would have been impossible in the early days because of lack of availability

18th century

- elegant colours of imported fabrics: blue, gold, soft red
- natural wood colours still
- muted tones of dried plant material
- bright mixed colours of fresh flowers as available
- no evidence of particular colour choice.

Containers

17th century

There were no special flower containers at this time.

Utensils brought from the old country could have been used. They would have been made of iron, pewter, brass, copper or wood in sturdy, simple shapes. Later, as craftsman began to arrive, simple pottery was made.

Kitchen utensil from early part of the period

Elegant, imported containers from later in the period

18th century

- imported containers made especially for flowers, e.g., salt glaze vases
- English creamware five-finger posy vases
- British pottery in blue and white, often a brick, also used for pens and ink
- Chinese export porcelain bowls
- crocus pots, glass bowls and tumblers
- Delftware
- Worcester and Chelsea porcelains
- Staffordshire earthenware vases

Mechanics

17th century

There were probably no mechanics, but flowers bunched together awaiting processing.

18th century

There was probably sand, twigs bunched together, or the flower stems packed tightly to support each other.

Suggested accessories

17th century

- homespun and dyed hand-woven fabric coverlets
- pewter mugs and plates
- wooden plates
- copper kettles
- long-handled iron dippers
- horn spoons
- muskets and rifles
- irons
- mat of hooked rags
- brass bed warmer
- cow's horn hooter
- betty lamp (an iron dish filled with oil or grease on which a wick floated)
- rush light with a clamp to hold straws or rushes dipped in fat for burning
- tin-glazed earthenware
- large, heavy Bible
- vellum-bound psalm book
- carved wooden chest
- homespun-linen valuables bag for carrying possessions to safety in the event of fire (a constant threat) or attack
- needlework

18th century

- patchwork quilts (would have been made in quilting parties)
- homespun linen embroidered with bright crewel-work
- pine clocks
- pine folding beds
- Turkish carpets
- eagle-stamped green glass bottles
- fine embroidery
- silver objects such as an inkstand, refashioned from silver coins (with no banks these were often stolen) to be easily identifiable
- any 17th- and 18th-century useful and decorative objects taken over or imported from the old country which can now be seen in our museums

References and resources

Plant material

Seeds, cuttings, roots and bulbs were imported and later the use of indigenous plants was learned from indigenous peoples. The three important herbals that were used were: John Gerard's *Herball* (1633 edition), John Parkinson's *Paradisi in Sole Paradisus Terrestris* (1629) and Nicholas Culpeper's *Herbal*.

Plants varied according to the location of the settlement and the climate. Full lists of the 17th- and 18th-century plants most frequently cultivated can be found in Ann Leighton's books – the accounts of the early surveyors, botanists, colonisers, historians and horticultural enthusiasts and books of medicines.

Flowers that were mentioned in *The Practical Farmer* (John Spurrier of Wilmington, 1793 are listed in Julia Berrall's *A History of Flower Arrangement* (The Studio Publications, 1953). She also notes relevant flowers from other sources.

Garden plants were grown for the survival of the family – as a general rule, the rural garden of this period was purely practical and designed in line with best horticultural practice. Plants that might be needed instantly, say for staunching a wound, were grown nearest the dwelling. Others were grouped according to whether they were perennials or annuals. Every plant had to flourish and every gardening effort had to be worthwhile because it took many weeks to import fresh seed from the 'old country'.

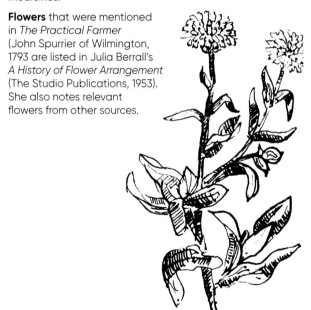

Double globe marigold, after an illustration in *Early English Gardens in New England* by Ann Leighton

17th-century plants

Achillea millefolium
Aconitum napellus
Allium ampeloprasum var. porrum
Allium sativum
Allium schoenoprasum
Althaea rosea Aquilegia vulgaris
Angelica archangelica
Antennaria howellii subsp. canadensis
Anthemis nobilis
Calendula officinalis
Cheiranthus cheiri syn. Erisimum cheiri
Chrysanthemum parthenium syn.
   Tanacetum parthenium
Cichorium endivia
Convallaria majalis
Cynara cardunculus Scolymus Group
Dianthus plumarius
Foeniculum vulgare
Galium verum
Helianthus tuberosus
Humulus lupulus
Inula helenium
Lavandula spica
Leucanthemum vulgare syn.
   Chrysanthemum leucanthemum
Lunaria annua
Matthiola sp.
Melissa officinalis
Mentha sp.
Nepeta cataria
Ocimum basilicum
Papaver somniferum
Petroselinum crispum
Polygonatum multiflorum
Prunus domestica
Prunus persica
Pyrus communis
Rosa sp.
Ruta graveolens
Salvia rosmarinus
Santolina chamaecyparissus
Thymus sp.
Tulipa sp.
Viola sp.

18th-century dried plants

Achillea millefolium
Allium moly
Amaranthus caudatus
Anaphalis margaritacea
   (pearly everlasting)
Angelica archangelica
Antennaria sp.
Capsicum annuum
Consolida ajacis syn. Delphinium ajacis
Cynara cardunculus Scolymus Group
Datura stramonium seed heads
Echinops ritro
Eryngium maritimum
Gomphrena globosa
Helianthus tuberosus
Helichrysum arenarium
Helichrysum petiolare
Humulus lupulus
Hydrangea arborescens
Lagenaria vulgaris
Lavandula spica
Limonium vulgare
Lunaria annua
Nigella damascena seed heads
Papaver orientale seed heads
Papaver somniferum seed heads
Punica granatum
Xeranthemum annuum
Xerochrysum bracteatum

Places to see

Museums and galleries

The American Museum & Gardens (Somerset). The many interesting features include rooms furnished in period style, a wonderful collection of quilts, a herb garden and shop.

Colonial Williamsburg Historic Area Virginia (USA)

V&A Museum (London)

Gardens

Quincy Homestead, Massachussetts (USA)

Tate House Museum, Maine (USA)

Whitehall Museum House, Rhode Island (USA)

There is a movement to recreate gardens of this era – many can be viewed online.

Georgian
1714–1830

RUTH HINTON

The period covers the reigns of the first four Georges and includes the Regency period after 1811.

Britain was affected by the French Revolution (1789) and the subsequent war against Napoleon, and by the loss of her American colonies after the war of American Independence in the 1770s. Despite this, the Georgian era was one of prosperity and is frequently called the 'Age of Elegance'. The craftsmanship of Georgian artists, musicians, cabinet makers, architects, silversmiths, writers and makers of porcelain has probably never been surpassed. The 'Grand Tour' was customary for the well-to-do and they brought back to England a taste for Chinese, Egyptian, Indian, Classical Greek and Roman styles.

Patronage of the arts flourished. Bath became the most fashionable town and 'taking the waters' there and at other spas was a fashionable pursuit: coffee houses were established; chocolate was a most popular drink; the 'promenade' was a feature in spas and parks and the elegance of the Regency bucks is legendary.

Fashionable town house of the period

How and where flowers were used

On side tables

Johann Zoffany royal portraits show vases of flowers near the sitter, usually on a side table.

Fireplaces

In summer, these featured bough pots with branches or flowers in fan-shaped display.

Vases

On mantelpieces, vases began to appear, either singly or as a pair, but paintings show the bouquets to be inconspicuous.

Delphiniums and roses from Zoffany's portrait of Queen Charlotte

On grand dining tables

A *surtout de table* or centrepiece was sometimes used, often with figurines of goddesses and cherubs holding garlands and with *parterres* of little hedges and decorative trees. These were sometimes of real plant material or of sugar confectionary. Pyramids of fruit decorated with leaves on low or compote dishes often flanked the surtout.

On the person

Flowers were worn as garlands on elaborately piled up hairstyles, pinned to the shoulder or bosom of a dress, and sometimes carried as a posy or in a basket.

Georgian silverware, such as this elegant 19th century épergne, remains unsurpassed

On walls

Vases or wall pockets held arrangements of flowers.

In bedrooms

Posies, of elongated shape rather than round were displayed.

Typical settings

Formal elegance and good proportions were key, especially in the Regency period. Chinoiserie settings were a cult in the mid-18th century and Chinese motifs appeared on silver, furniture, bronzes, wallpapers and porcelain. Natural forms were used in ornamental plasterwork and carving, e.g., *Rosa, Lonicera*, in the stylized *anthemion* motif (a design of alternating motifs resembling clusters of narrow leaves or honeysuckle petals), *Garrya elliptica* catkins and scallop shells. Upholstery was mainly in floral patterned silk and damask or tapestry, but also in heavy cotton printed in blue, red and sepia with plant forms and scenes (*toile de Jouy*). Woods used were mainly walnut, mahogany and satinwood, later with inlays or painted borders and medallions.

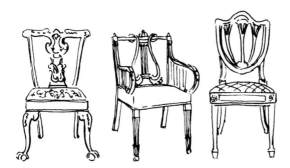

Chairs by Chippendale, Adam and Hepplewhite

Other popular settings:

- Palladian (Italian) style archways, columns and porticos
- tapestries in Gobelin style, with floral garlands, swags and arrangements in urns, with pictures of scenes from classical legends
- elegant Chippendale, Hepplewhite and Sheraton furniture
- Adam-style interiors in grey-green, pink or blue, with white carved plasterwork friezes, ceilings, door pediments and fireplace surrounds, often with fruit and flower motifs
- gilt arabesques in frames to mirrors and mantelpieces and in wall sconces
- artist-designed or imported wallpapers with stripes, floral bands, baskets of flowers, ribbons, bows and pastoral scenes
- fireplaces in white marble with caryatids and interesting fireboards

Textiles

By the 18th century, a great variety of fabrics was available.

Spitalfields' silks were popular as well as those imported from the East.

Also: mohair, plush velvet both plain and patterned, moreen, watered silk, damask of silk or cotton, printed cotton (including toile de Jouy), chintz, satin, brocade, taffeta and Brussels and Gobelin tapestries.

Fabrics were embroidered, usually with floral motifs, for clothes, wall panels and drapes, bedcovers and hangings, cushions.

Flowers from embroidered coverlet in V&A Museum

Symbolism

There is virtually no evidence of plant symbolism being important during this period.

Overall characteristics of the period

The early Georgian style was Baroque, and paintings by Jan van Huysum show arrangements similar to middle period Dutch/Flemish flower pieces. Colours at this time are rich and glowing, but there is more restraint and control in the design.

The second half of the 18th century shows first the influence of French Rococo lightness and delicacy, and secondly classical restraint and elegance. By the time of the Regency era, all these influences combined to produce a delicate, controlled elegance which has, nevertheless, a quality of richness about it. In flower arrangements this is often achieved by the use of hothouse flowers and blooms of perfection.

Some monochromatic colouring was used, but more usually, mixed arrangements of clear and pastel colours such as apricot, cream, blue, mauve, rose-pink, and grey-green. Brighter and deeper colours are included but the general effect is never heavy or garish.

Overall balance is generally symmetrical, though interest is often achieved by asymmetrical detail within the design. Flowers are arranged loosely and, although massed, they are not packed without space.

Colour

- Decoratively, colours were clear, but more subtle than previously.
- The grey-blues and grey-greens of Wedgewood and Adam were popular.
- Clear red, dark rich green, Chinese yellow, strawberry pink, turquoise, peach, apricot and cream.
- Adam style decoration showed touches of deep rust, soft mushroom and burnt sienna.
- Georgian colouring may have been pastel, sometimes bright, but never gaudy.

Containers

Porcelain and pottery bough pots, bowls, urns, tall vases often with handles and lids and in pairs; flower bricks, wall vases or 'pockets' in cornucopia shapes, root pots, baskets, shell-shaped and five-fingered vases – all made by the famous porcelain factories in Bow, Derby and Staffordshire and elsewhere, or were imported from China.

A five-fingered vase

From Robert Furber's *Twelve Months of Flowers* (1730). Designed by Pieter Casteels, the illustrations show flowers arranged in urns and other containers

Wedgewood Jasperware also came in many shapes, with raised white classical decoration on blue, sage-green, lilac-pink or black background.

Treen tazzas, urns and goblets; in glass-tumbler shapes and hyacinth vases and in wicker baskets.

Bases

Vases often incorporated their own bases or had matching plinths or stands, often tiered and footed.

Table centrepieces usually had their own 'plateau', or base frequently covered with mirror glass and edged with a gallery.

Jasper vase
Wedgewood (1790)

Mechanics

Many bowls and vases of this period had their own perforated tops to hold flowers (or quill pens), or perforated plates which fitted the top of the container. Moss and sand were probably also used to support stems.

Containers often had perforated tops to hold flowers

Suggested accessories

As flower arrangements stood on mantelpieces and side tables, any Georgian ornament, especially in porcelain or silver, would be appropriate. An 18th-century widower wrote of the bunch of fresh flowers he always kept in his study by a portrait of his wife.

Georgian bric-a-brac might include:

- animals or groups of animals
- bell pulls
- birds on a branch
- candlesticks with snuffers or trimmers
- inkstands
- orange bowls with covers
- pastille burners in the form of cottages or castles
- porcelain cameos
- porcelain figures of street sellers
- potpourri vases
- redware tea caddies
- scent bottles
- shepherds and shepherdesses
- snuff and patch boxes
- spill vases and match pots

References and resources

Plant material

The Georgians used both fresh and dried flowers: *Lunaria annua, Xerochrysum bracteum, Gomphrena globosa* etc.

Hannah Glasse, writing in 1800 in *The Complete Confectioner* about table decorations says, "you must have artificial flowers of all sorts... and some natural from out of the garden in summer do very well intermixed".

Because gardens were landscaped largely without flowers, hot-house flowers were popular, both cut and growing in pots, for indoor decoration. The emphasis was on quality of bloom.

Flowers
18th-century writers mention:
Aconitum sp.
Agave amica syn. *Polianthes tuberose'*
Antirrhinum sp.
Campanula sp.
Convallaria majalis
Delphinium sp.
Dianthus caryophyllus
Hesperis matronalis
Iris sp.
Lathyrus odoratus
Lilium sp.
Paeonia sp.
Philadelphus sp.
Syringa sp.
Reseda odorata
Rosa banksiae 'Lutea'
Viburnum opulus 'Roseum'

To enumerate all available would be impossible, but Jan van Huysum's *Twelve Months of Flowers* series of paintings depict many others, including:
Amaryllis
Anemone
Calendula
Crocus
Geranium
Helleborus
Hyacinthus
Jasminum
Myosotis
Narcissus
Nerine
Phlox
Prunus
Scabiosa
Tulipa (variegated and striped flowers)
Veronica
Viola

The *Auricula* was a special favourite and the growing and breeding of it a craze similar to the tulip mania of the 17th century. This illustration interprets a description of an Auricula Theatre from Rowland Biffen's *The Auricula*

Foliage

Arrangements, unless of branches in bough pots did not contain a great deal of added foliage but, where needed, the following could be used in addition to the leaves of the flowers listed:

Artemisia sp.
Aucuba japonica
Bergenia sp.
Camellia sp.
Cytisus sp.
Enkianthus sp.
Erica sp.
Euonymus sp.
Hosta sp.
Hydrangea sp.
Kalmia sp.
Ligustrum sp.
Magnolia sp.
Mahonia sp.
Pieris sp.
Rhododendron sp.
Ruta sp.
Salvia rosmarinus
Vitis sp.
Wisteria sp.
Yucca sp.

Edible fruits

18th-century grand houses featured orangeries, so oranges and lemons were often homegrown, as well as grapes, melons, figs, pomegranates, peaches, nectarines and apricots, in addition to the fruits of the more temperate English climate: apples, cherries, currants, pears, plums, quinces, mulberries, blackberries, raspberries, gooseberries and strawberries.

Places to see

Georgian houses and streets are well-preserved in Bath, Brighton, Edinburgh, around London's Regent's Park and in many smaller towns.

Georgian architecture, interiors and furnishings can be seen in many grand houses open to the public. These include:

Blenheim Palace (Oxfordshire), Bowood House (Wiltshire), Castle Howard (Yorkshire), Clandon Park (Surrey), Harewood House (West Yorkshire), Keddlestone Hall (Derbyshire), Kenwood House (London), Newby Hall (North Yorkshire), Osterley Park (London), Saltram House (Devon), Syon Park (London), Uppark (West Sussex) and others.

Landscaped gardens can be seen in their mature beauty at Burghley House (Cambridgeshire), Holkham Hall (Norfolk), Petworth House (West Sussex), Stowe (Buckinghamshire), and Stourhead (Wiltshire).

Pictures of the age hang in the National, Tate and National Portrait galleries in London, the National Gallery of Scotland (Edinburgh) and in many others. Mrs Delany's paper mosaic flower pictures are in the British Museum (London).

Historic publications

There are many books on Georgian furniture, silver, porcelain and glass, which can provide useful background information and inspiration.

Rococo

1715–1774

ADELE GOTOBED

The term Rococo stems from the French words *rocailles* (rocks) and *coquilles* (shells), which were used for decoration in France from the 16th century onwards. The style borrowed freely from nature using flower, leaf, rock and shell forms on carved, painted, ceramic and metal ornaments.

Cleverly twisting lines from shells and scrolls characterize the style

Having evolved from the heavier Baroque style, it was essentially asymmetrical and free flowing and well suited to the less formal, smaller residences, rooms and salons favoured by the French nobility after the death of Louis XIV.

This was a time of peace before the storms of war and revolution. It was contemporary with the reign of George I, George II and part of the reign of George III in England. The court, wearied by stately formality and solemnity, was ready for change. The new heir was only five years old and the Regent, Philip, Duke of Orleans, was a person of culture, a great lover of the art and a setter of fashion with an appetite for gaiety. He quickly engendered an outburst of high living continued by Louis XV when he came to the throne in 1723.

In 1742 Louis met Madame de Pompadour who, with her strong character and many and varied talents, did much to influence the development of the Louis XV style. A patron of the arts, she befriended a wide variety of writers, artists and artisans including Voltaire, Boucher, her court painter and custodian of the Gobelin tapestries, and the humble decorators of Sèvres porcelain. The famous Petit Trianon chateau at Versailles was created for her by Louis.

How and where flowers were used

- on mantels, console tables, commodes, lampadaires (tripod pedestals)
- on walls in wall pockets and cornucopia

On grand dining tables

As Margaret Marcus records in *Period Flower Arrangement* (Barrows, 1952), "Floral settings for banquets, small parties, buffet suppers and picnics were most elaborate. Ornaments for table settings included towering épergnes with containers for foliage, fruit and sweetmeats, architectural structures and ceramic figures.

"Table sets sometimes included three hundred pieces, amongst them domed temples, arches, épergnes, arbours embellished with trees, branches and flowers, vases, girandoles, candlesticks and china figures. Symmetrical pyramids of fruit often stood at intervals down the length of banqueting table."

On the person

Chaplets were worn on the head; garlands across the chest from shoulder to waist, around the upper arm; sprays were worn on one shoulder or on the bosom.

Typical settings

Interiors were decorated in closely related hues. The style has remained popular and today, you can still find wallpapers and fabrics reminiscent of the period with Chinese, mythological or pastoral scenes, and in style of *toile de Jouy*.

- buildings in fine, greyish-yellow stone; graceful town houses free from columns and pilasters
- French windows which allowed daylight to flood in and play across decorated interiors
- carved wooden panels in gilded stucco with garlands
- splendid glass chandeliers and mirrors in carved frames usually gilded, fitted with tapestries and fine embroideries
- commodes with carved legs and coloured marble tops
- screens with richly carved frames, usually gilded, fitted with tapestries or fine embroideries
- tapestries made at Gobelin, Beauvais and Aubusson featuring mythological or hunting scenes; many incorporating flowers in urns, swags and basket.
- chinoiseries including furniture, screens, chests and porcelain, frequently lacquered, decorated with ormolu and/or gilded bronze
- porcelain from many famous factories, particularly Sèvres with its base colours of dark and turquoise blues, apple-green, *rose Pompadour* (pink), decorated with flowers, landscapes, baskets of flowers and bowknots, nymphs and shepherds
- elegant furniture in light coloured woods with marquetry featuring bouquets of flowers, landscapes, trophies of war, musical instruments and shepherds' crooks hung with ribbons
- paintings portraying pastoral scenes and images of love

Textiles

In this elegant age there was a wealth of choice. Tapestries were available from the factories of Gobelin, Beauvais, Savonnerie with carpets from Aubusson.

Rich silks came from the mills of Lyons and were imported from China. They were used for wall hangings, upholstery and cushions.

Specially designed fabrics were made for furniture, usually in floral patterns, seldom plain, in damask, velvet, brocade of petit point.

Curtains were of patterned silk and velvet; table covers often in satin.

Toile de Jouy, linen or cotton printed with pastoral scenes in a single colour on a light background, was popular after 1760.

Armchair fauteuil (c1740)

Design for a tapestry panel – Louis XVI period

Symbolism

There is no evidence of plant symbolism during this period.

Overall characteristics of the period

Rococo is the least weighty of all mass arrangements, with harmony rather than contrast in the soft colourings. Spiky flowers and trailing tendrils are used in a graceful manner, and the individual beauty of the flowers is stressed. Design should seldom be absolutely symmetrical (except in the case of pyramids of fruit), and many feature asymmetrical S and C curves. Proportions vary. The height of flowers in basket and urns is sometimes less than the height of the container, sometimes about equal and in some stately vases, graceful stems are twice the height of the vase. Paintings by Gerard van Spaendonck and Anna Vallayer-Coster, although rather late for the period, show how the Rococo style continued to influence arrangements.

Colour

Examples of colour can be found on porcelain and tapestry though, in the latter, colours may have faded with age.

- Mainly delicate, pastel colours used, such as shell-pink, pale and golden yellows, blue-green, turquoise, light blue with accents of dark blue and violet, warm tones of grey, warm tones of orange, apricot and cream.
- Colours should be selected for subtle harmonious effect such as are found on the inside of shells.
- Chinese lacquerware influenced the use of green, gold, touches of red and of course, black.
- Gilding was frequently used.

Assymetrical arrangement

Containers

Motifs on containers as well as furniture and ornaments included lion masks, rams' heads, dolphins, swags and friezes of fruit and flowers, acanthus scrolls, sunbursts, scallop shells and rosettes.

- urns of all types, tall, medium, wide-mouthed; of classical lines; usually with handles; in metal, marble or porcelain; frequently ornamented with carved, moulded or painted scenes
- baskets, both tall and low, oval or round, in open-work porcelain, silver or reed
- bowls of Chinese porcelain, malachite or other stone often mounted in ormolu
- wall pockets and cornucopia, usually of porcelain
- flower bricks and square vases fitted with holes for flower stems also bulb holders
- épergnes in many materials and sizes especially for table decorations

Typical containers of the period

Bases

Many containers, especially urns incorporated plinths to match, often fitted with animal feet or leaf curls.

Mechanics

The whole style of Rococo was to celebrate the natural, so there was a move away from using specific mechanics other than the support provided by vases and containers.

Suggested accessories

Items seen in paintings include: lace fans, candelabra, candlesticks (ormolu, Dresden or Sèvres), porcelain birds, figurines and flowers, decorative snuff and patch boxes of painted enamel or Sèvres, jewel cases, miniatures, embroidery frames, baskets for tatting bobbins and thread, marble or bronze busts or statues, ornamental clocks, decorative hand mirrors, pomade jars, French prints, nosegays tied with ribbon.

Corner cabinet with bronze curving Rococo decorations

Chiselled gilt-bronze candlestick with asymmetrical design (c1745)

References and resources

Plant material

Flowers (mentioned by writers or seen in paintings)
Acacia
Agave amica syn. *Polianthes tuberose*
Althaea
Anemone
Antirrhinum
Aster
Auricula
Bellis perennis
Campanula medium
Centaurea cyanus
Citrus bergamia blossom
Clematis
Consolida ajacis (syn. *Delphinium ajacis*)
Convallaria majalis
Convolvulus
Crocus
Dianthus caryophyllus
Fritillaria imperialis
Fritillaria meleagris
Gladiolus (dark purple with white centre stripe)
Helleborus niger
Hyacinthus
Ipomoea
Iris
Jasminum
Lilium candidum
Lilium umbellatum
Lonicera
Matthiola
Narcissus
Paeonia
Papaver (and seed head)
Prunus blossom (including double)
Prunus dulcis blossom
Ranunculus
Rosa x *centifolia*
Rosa x *damascena*
Rosa gallica
Syringa
Tanacetum vulgare
Tulipa
Viburnum opulus 'Roseum'
Viola

Foliage
There is little evidence of added foliage. In most cases leaves are of the flowers used at the time, frequently selected for design quality e.g., *Paeonia*, *Papaver* and *Rosa*.

Edible fruits
Pineapple was the king of fruits in the 18th century, replacing the melon which was popular in the 17th century. At Easter pineapples constructed of daffodils and crowned with their own foliage, were sold in the streets to decorate the breakfast table.
Orangeries were a feature of the grand houses of this period so that for most exotic fruit such as peaches, apricots, grapes, nectarines, oranges, melons and strawberries were available. Outdoor grown fruits included apples, cherries, gooseberries, quinces, mulberries and pears.

Gardens

French gardens, which had been formal and symmetrical in Louis XIV's time with elaborate parterres, topiary, statuary, water and fountains, became more naturalistic and were landscaped 'in English style'. Winding paths and romantic ruins set off by clumps of specimen trees were designed in the Rococo manner for agreeable outdoor enjoyment rather than ostentatious pageantry. Flowers for indoor decoration were still mainly grown in the *jardin fleuriste* or cutting garden. One bitterly cold winter, Madame de Pompadour filled the flower beds of one of her gardens with porcelain flowers and sprinkled scent in the air to complete the illusion.

Places to see

Museums and galleries

Lady Lever Art Gallery (Merseyside) – Gobelin tapestry, furniture and paintings

V&A Museum (London) – 18th-century continental rooms

Wallace Collection (London) – unsurpassed French 18th-century painting (including Old Masters), furniture, porcelain and a world class armoury

Historic buildings and monuments

Blenheim Palace (Oxfordshire), furniture

Claydon (Buckinghamshire), the dining room

Cliveden (Buckinghamshire), the North Hall

Harewood House (West Yorkshire), Chinese porcelain with ormolu

Luton Hoo (Bedfordshire), tapestries in the Blue Hall

Newby Hall (North Yorkshire), Gobelin tapestries

Painswick Gardens (Gloucestershire)

Woburn Abbey (Bedfordshire), Sèvres dinner service and settings

Victorian

1837–1901

EDNA BARLOW

This was the era of the Industrial Revolution with a vast increase in economic wealth and the rise of the middle classes. Britain became 'the workshop of the world'. The British Empire was at the height of its power. Patriotism was widespread and fashionable.

While poorer women were employed in domestic service or in mills and factories, young ladies were expected to be accomplished in all household arts and crafts. The social structure was well defined and everyone 'knew his place'. Manufactured goods in profusion encouraged clutter as never before.

This was a romantic period – sentimental, outwardly pious and strictly moral, concerned with death and mourning, and with a deep reverence later in the century for queen and country.

How and where flowers were used

In the house

As today, flowers were used anywhere and everywhere. Occasional tables, mantelpieces, fireplaces and cabinets featured the massed oval shape in a vase. Growing plants were massed in fireplaces in summer, in corners of rooms and halls, and complete arbours were made around sofas or doorways.

Fireplace with ferns

Skeletonized flowers and leaves, known as phantoms, were displayed against black velvet; dried flowers covered in white wax were often used as memorials; immortelles or strawflowers were used to frame pictures and to make everlasting wreaths.

Even fresh flowers were put under glass domes, and Wardian cases of growing plants were used in a variety of sizes and designs.

Wardian cases

Decorated dinner table

On dining tables

- characteristically an elaborate, massed centrepiece in an *épergne* or March stand
- cone-shaped bouquets, one for each guest, piled at the base
- fruits often in pyramids on separate compotes, edged with a frill of leaves
- trailing foliage such as *Smilax*, *Hedera* and *Asparagus* fern were laid directly on the table or scroll and scallop patterns made with separate leaves or evergreen *Hedera* or *Pelargonium*
- for banquets and special occasions, or a scene to reflect the occasion, such as an Indian scene or Arab camp to honour a soldier

On the person

Flowers were worn in the hair as wreaths or single flowers; carried in the hand as a posy or bouquet; festooned on skirts; used as corsages or shoulder ornaments or in a 'bosom bottle' at the neck of a dress.

In churches

Lavish decorations, mainly with foliage and pot plants, at Christmas and other festivals. At the wedding of Princess Beatrice in July 1885, at Whippingham, Isle of Wight, the church was decorated with foliage and pyramids of flowers in pots.

Typical settings

- cluttered, comfortable, over-stuffed rooms
- crocheted and hand worked doilies, mats and antimacassars
- curtains of lace and velvet, plush, chenille and baize trimmed with braid, bobble and other fringes, looped and tied back with cords and tassels
- dining tables usually covered in white damask, perhaps with coloured gauze or silk under the centrepiece
- flock-patterned wallpaper, especially in red and green
- flowers made of wax, wool, silk, leather, hair, feathers, shells, beads and seaweed, as framed pictures or under glass domes
- the library, smoking-room, study, billiards-room and conservatory were features of the houses of the 'nouveau-riche'
- oil-lamps, candlesticks and gas-lamp brackets
- ornate marble fireplaces and mantelpieces, with black-leaded grates and fire-irons and elaborate overmantels
- painted lincrusta-style wallpaper in raised patterns
- religious pictures and texts; paintings 'telling a story'
- stained glass panels
- symmetrical arrangements of furniture and ornaments usually in pairs
- tables, boxes, shelves, 'what-nots', cupboards and chests in mahogany, rosewood, walnut, bamboo, papier-mâché with mother-of-pearl decorations, marquetry, inlays and carving

Symbolism and meanings

The language of flowers

Every flower had a meaning. Bouquets were put together to convey messages which could be interpreted by published sign manuals. Ladies kept albums often painted in water-colours. Lovers sent messages in this manner and sympathy in bereavement was also expressed.

Symbolism in trees

The weeping forms of many trees were planted as mourning symbols. Queen Victoria's obsession with mourning in her widowhood was copied in all strata of society. Weeping ash, elm birch, cypress, spruce, *Sophora* and willow were popular. A high death rate made grief a familiar part of Victorian lives. Memorial pictures featuring a broken column and a weeping tree were worked in the hair of the deceased.

Symbolism on tombs

Carved in marble or stone, poppy heads signified 'sleep'; a rosebud with a broken stem – a child; wheat – old age; a bridal wreath severed by a dart – a bride cut down. *Hedera* stood for persistent life amid death. It was used everywhere, outlining doors, archways and windows; draped or grown around stairways and bannisters; festooned over portraits and busts, and long shoots were even introduced for house decoration from plants growing outside a window. Queen Victoria, a young wife, wore a wreath of real Osborne *Hedera*, intermingled with diamonds, in her hair.

Pressed mementoes

The sentimental pressing of flowers and leaves from bouquets or special occasions, or as souvenirs of holidays or friends, was carried out by almost every woman.

Overall characteristics of the period

The main characteristic is massed flowers and foliage, with little space and no obvious centre of interest. The shape is oval or circular and the height of the flowers often less than that of the container.

Vases usually held massed bouquets of mixed flowers, sometimes with trailing ferns and greenery.

Posies of concentric circles of flowers were popular for carrying in the hand.

Posy of concentric circles

One desciption of a Victorian bouquet in 1850 reads:
"Take the largest red rose or the palest lily for the centre feature. With coarse thread fasten this to a small stick. Holding the stick in the left hand, lash to it a series of flower circles – each blossom round a contrast to the preceding one. Occasionally you may wish to insert a few sprigs of grasses, lashing all tightly. When you have obtained the desired size, set off the bouquet with a ruffle of small scented or feathery leaves i.e. smilax, geranium, southernwood or myrtle …."

Colour

The first aniline dye (violet) was produced in 1856. After that colours tended to be harsh and strident. Contrasts were preferred to harmonies. The harsh medley of the 'carpet-bedding' of flowers in the garden was repeated indoors with magenta, puce, heliotrope, harsh red and green, acid yellow, mustard, dark brown, 'faded' navy blue, dark crimson, mulberry, maroon and 'carnation pink' (a violent hue favoured by the Empress Eugenie).

"There is no doubt that arranging flowers according to their contrast or complementary colours is more pleasing to the eye than placing them according to their harmonies ... Consequently, a blue flower should be placed next to an orange, a yellow near violet and a red or white should have plants with abundant foliage near them" – (from *Window Gardening – Devoted Specially to the Culture of Flowers and Ornamental Plants for Indoor Use and Parlour Decoration* c. 1870.)

Containers

To quote Margaret Marcus from *Period Flower Arrangements* (Barrows, 1952), containers were of ".... all conceivable and inconceivable shapes".

Hand vase

Baskets in every sort of material, vases in the form of hands, boots, boats, animals and birds, shells, buildings and monuments, Indian brass, Chinese blue and white porcelain, ginger jars and so on.

Epergnes, also known as March stands or Ellen Terry stands, usually consisted of cornet-shaped flower containers grouped round a tall central one, in glass, silver, alabaster or other metal, generally about 60cm high; flower holders were often in the shape of *Lilium* or *Convolvulus*.

Epergne

March stand

Glass containers were in every shape and cut, blown, etched, moulded and pressed; clear, coloured, milk, gilded, painted and enamelled; raised decoration in a different coloured glass was popular, often in shell patterns or barley-sugar twists.

Posy holders or *porte-bouquets* were designed to be carried in the hand or clipped to the dress to protect the flowers from hot hands and were usually cornet-shaped and made from crystal, porcelain, enamel, gold and silver filigree, set with jewels and often a mother-of-pearl handle. A small pin on a short chain anchored the posy in place, and a ring on a chain allowed it to dangle when the wearer was dancing.

Vases and urns in a variety of shapes were in porcelain, sometimes hand-painted with applied modelling, in alabaster, marble and metal including spelter; tall containers usually had narrow necks.

Arrangement in tall glass vase with paper frill

Posy holder

Bases

- crocheted and lace-edged doilies, often in white, cream and ecru
- embroidered mats in Berlin work, a form of wool cross-stitch
- moss mats crocheted in green and brown wool to simulate moss
- Many ornaments had their own base of ebonized wood, with small feet or round knobs

Mechanics

- glass or pottery 'roses' with holes to hold stems
- specimen vases for one or two flowers
- wet and dry sand and moss
- wire mesh frames or perforated lids fitted to bowls and vases
- wire spirals on a base
- In churches, rope, wire or thin lathes of wood were used for garlands.
- shapes were made of perforated wood or zinc, or of wire mesh over a light wooden frame, and foliage was either glued on, inserted through the holes or stitched on with dark green thread

glass 'rose'

Spiral wires on metal base

Suggested accessories

Accessories were probably not used consciously at the time, but flowers would have stood among the clutter of a Victorian parlour or living room. For period atmosphere the following would be suitable:

- bellpull
- bible, religious text
- Bristol blue or cranberry glass
- chatelaine
- coloured glass paperweight
- commemorative pottery/trinket
- decorated vase
- embroidered sampler
- fan, dance card
- family photograph (faded sepia)
- holiday mementoes
- jet/silver/mother-of-pearl ornaments
- kitchen utensils of period
- locket and chain, brooch
- lustre vase
- mourning cards/handkerchief
- portrait of Queen Victoria
- shell-covered box

References and resources

Plant material

Flowers
This was an exciting period for plant lovers, with clipper ships bringing:

Canna sp.
Dahlia sp.
Forsythia sp.
Fuchsia sp.
Gloxinia sp.
Lamprocapnos (syn. *Dicentra*)
Salvia sp.
Wisteria sp.
Geranium sp. and *Lobelia* sp. came from Africa and *Petunia* sp. from Mexico.

The Victorians also used:
Antirrhinum sp.
Bellis perennis
Calceolaria sp.
Calendula sp.
Camellia sp., the supreme flower for decoration after Dumas' play *La Dame aux Camellias*
Celosia argentea var. *cristata*
Chrysanthemum sp.
Consolida ajacis syn. *Delphinium ajacis*
Convallaria majalis
Convolvulus sp.
Crocosmia sp.
Dianthus sp., 'Empire Daisy'
Erysimum cheiri, a favourite of Prince Albert
Hosta sp.
Hyacinthus sp.
Iberis umbellate
Galanthus sp.
Gladiolus sp.
Lathyrus odoratus
Lilium sp.
Lunaria sp
Matthiola sp.
Narcissus sp.
Paeonia sp.
Papaver sp.
Passiflora sp.
Phlox sp.
Polyanthus sp.
Primula sp.
Ranunculus sp.
Reseda sp. (mignonette)
Rosa sp.
Scilla sp.
Tulipa sp.
Viola sp.

Foliage
Foliage of all kinds was used including variegated and grey-leaved. *Hedera* and ferns were especially popular – there was a 'fern craze' between the 1840s and 1860s. Dark evergreens such as *Cupressus* sp., *Ilex* sp., *Laurus* sp., *Myrtus communis* and *Taxus baccata* were typical of Victorian shrubberies. *Aralia* sp., *Arundinaria* sp., *Acanthus* sp. and *Garrya* sp. also. Exotic foliages such as *Caladium* sp., *Codiaeum* sp., *Dracaena* sp. and *Maranta* sp. were grown in the conservatory, greenhouse or Wardian case. Potted palms and *Aspidistra elatior* plants were commonplace.

Edible fruits
All the English fruits were available and in hothouses and conservatories of large houses, grapes, nectarines, oranges, peaches and pineapples.

Grass
Grasses of every type, both wild and cultivated, were used in floral decoration and the striped leaves of *Phalaris arundinacea* var. *picta* (gardeners' garters), were popular.

Immortelles
Immortelles – everlasting flowers were in vogue, e.g., species of *Acroclinum, Rhodanthe, Xeranthemum* and *Xerochrysum* syn. *Helichrysum*.

People to look up

Gardeners

Gertrude Jekyll (1843-1932)

John Loudon (1783-1843) and his wife, Jane (1807-1858) who wrote about gardening for ladies

Joseph Paxton (1803-1865) who designed the Crystal Palace

William Robinson (1838-1935) said to have invented 'modern' gardening

James Veitch (1815-1869) who sent plant hunters all over the world

Nathaniel Ward (1791-1868) the London physician who invented the Wardian case

Artists and craftsmen

Peter Carl Fabergé (1846-1920), master jeweller

Charles Rennie Mackintosh (1868-1928), architect and designer

William Morris (1834-1896), designer

Places to see

Museums and galleries

Museum of the Home (London) features rooms furnished in period style

V&A Museum (London) exhibits many aspects of Victorian life

York Castle Museum (North Yorkshire)

Historic buildings and monuments

A La Ronde (Devon)

Calke Abbey (Derbyshire)

Cragside House (Northumberland)

Linley Sambourne House (London)

Wightwick Manor (late Victorian home, Warwickshire)

Gardens

Biddulph Grange, (Staffordshire)

Bodnant Garden, Conwy (Wales)

Cragside (Northumberland)

Garden squares, particularly in London in Belgravia, Bloomsbury, Brompton, Cadogan Place, Kensington, Notting Hill

Gawthorpe Hall (Lancashire)

Hughenden (Buckinghamshire)

Peckover House and Garden (Cambridgeshire)

Royal Botanic Gardens, Kew, (London) for the Palm House

Rowallane Garden (County Down)

Scotney Castle (Kent)

See also

carpet-bedding as still carried out in many parks

antique white-painted wrought iron garden furniture

Victorian facades of many railway stations

Edwardian and Art Nouveau

1890–1914

ANNE BOASE

The Edwardian era, typified by such phrases as the 'naughty nineties', The Belle Epoque, fin de siècle and the long summer, was less formal, more spacious and elegant than the preceding Victorian period.

The well-to-do spent lavishly and lived extravagantly, but the emergence of the Labour Party, trades unions and the suffragette movement showed the stirrings of a social conscience over the poverty of the working classes.

Electricity in the home, the telephone and motorcars, were beginning to transform everyday life. Department stores boomed; sport – cricket, tennis, football, croquet, swimming and golf, theatres, music halls, fairs, circuses, working men's clubs and public houses provided entertainment for both rich and poor.

Typical Art Nouveau poster style

The decorative style known as Art Nouveau swept through Europe and America – a revolt against the crude mass products and designs of the late 19th century. In England, William Morris and the Pre-Raphaelite movement paved the way. Typical of Art Nouveau are stylised, sinuous plant forms with a whiplash design of stems, female figures with flowing hair and draperies and cleverly contrived 'wilful asymmetry', as the art historian James Laver called it. The style was in evidence in furniture and buildings as well as in posters, lampshades, ornaments and dress.

How and where flowers were used

Flower vases and bowls were used throughout the house – on tables, sills, chests, mantelpieces and pianos.

Dining tables

Elaborately festooned tables were still used for grand occasions, much as in the latter Victorian era but, generally, table decoration was simpler than it had been. The 'new' electric table lamps usually had shades made of silk and often had arrangements at the base with a few flowers of the same kind pinned to the shade.

Robert Felton writing in his *British Floral Decoration* (A & C Black, 1910) offered this on table decoration; "although it is always advisable when decorating a small or large table to employ one kind of flower, or at most two, it is quite possible to make exquisite colour schemes of a great number of flowers". He goes on to advise that, "if you have a tall centre you should also have fairly tall end-pieces with low ones between them..." and that "during the last ten years we have abolished masses of coloured gauze, ribbons, silk table centres and with the French and German methods, mirrors, epergnes and many other abominations have ceased to exist".

Gertrude Jekyll garden designer, writer and associate of Sir Edwin Lutyens, the architect, published *Flower Decoration in the House* in 1907 and introduced more modern ideas into flower arrangement. Her preference was for markedly asymmetrical groupings of tall vases with low bowls or taller jugs balancing low placements of fruit, as seen in the illustration. Hogarth curves are traceable in many of her designs and a strong sense of colour-toning is evident.

Munstead Wood, Godalming, Surrey built by Edward Lutyens for Miss Gertrude Jekyll in 1897

Art Nouveau influences simplified flower arrangements even further. Pictures of tearooms in Glasgow designed by Charles Rennie Mackintosh show simple vases arranged with just a few flowers in Ikebana style on tables, sills and mantelshelves. In other houses designed by Mackintosh, there were simple vases of branches of blossom or coloured twigs – a very far cry from the excesses of Victoriana.

Fruit simply arranged on a pewter dish with vine and fig foliage – by Gertrude Jekyll (1907)

William Robinson author of *The English Flower Garden* (John Murray, 1921) has a chapter on flowers in the house: "a large flat bowl can look attractive showing a certain expanse of water and two or three spikes of iris, or similar flowers standing at one side", as "the art of flower arrangement comes from making a lot from a little material and calls for artistry as well as taste".

Flowers were extensively worn by ladies with afternoon and evening dress as a corsage or at the waist and gentlemen favoured buttonholes.

Mrs Beeton whose writing continued to be popular in this period, advocated simple and inexpensive decorations including grasses, water lilies (mentioned by nearly all writers), primroses and cowslips, autumn-tinted foliage, pressed golden bracken and ferns in shells or little rustic baskets.

Table decorations – *Mrs Beeton's Cookery Book* (1895)

Typical settings

Furniture was much less ornate and rooms less cluttered than in Victorian times with fewer ornaments and knick-knacks. Fireplaces lost their heavy overmantels and simpler wood surroundings were more in keeping with Art Nouveau influences. Silver, silver plate, pewter and decorated enamel wares were much used along with decorated enamel.

- wallpapers and fabrics designed by William Morris, C A Voysey and Walter Crane
- large, blowsy roses on wallpaper
- satinwood is distinctive of the period, so also is oak, ash hazel birch, stained pine and walnut rather than mahogany
- cream and white painted woodwork.
- lace and later, net curtains; vibrant cretonne loose covers and curtains
- standard lamps, pianos and mirrors were almost essential furnishings
- stained glass panels in doors, windows and bookcases, screens etc.
- lampshades in silk with beads or fringes, or made from coloured glass
- posters of the era (now popular again)
- gramophones with 'morning glory' trumpets, as in 'His Master's Voice'

Edwardian drawing-room

Tiffany tree form lamp – green and purple fruit, violet leaves

Oxidised silver electric light pendant with opal glass shades (1913)

High-backed chair in dark stained oak by Charles Rennie Mackintosh (1897)

Symbolism

The Victorian language of flowers continued to be popular during the Edwardian period, but interest gradually declined and the First World War naturally brought about a more realistic attitude to flowers. The rose, usually stylized, was a widespread Art Nouveau motif and Art Nouveau designers often used flowers for their medieval and legendary associations.

Overall characteristics of the period

The tightly massed Victorian style gave way gradually to lighter arrangements of, often, one kind of flower with its own foliage and *Gypsophila* or *Asparagus setaceus*.

The influence of Ikebana was seen in the simple Art Nouveau arrangements of perhaps five or seven flowers of one kind with their own foliage.

The important thing was to be tasteful; writers of the time repeatedly referred to good taste and are scornful of the excesses of the Victorians. Toning colours and harmonious colour combinations began to be important, though Robert Felton lists many contrasts which he found successful – scarlet and white; yellow, bronze and pale mauve; plum and yellow and salmon pink with lilac. Church decoration was still rather heavy.

Colour

The iridescent, mother-of-pearl, butterfly wing look was popular. The whole range of colours was more subtle and greyed that the crude hues of the Victorians. Grey-green, green-gold, olive, lilac, turquoise, pearl-grey, burnt orange, bronze, fawn, eau-de-nil, rose-pink, cream-black and white, as in the famous Ascot scene in *My Fair Lady*, were all used in furnishings and in dress.

Colour combinations too were more subtle, with variations preferred to contrasts and there was much more attempt at colour matching. The emphasis was on tasteful rather than dramatic colour harmonies. The period has been described by some as probably the last age of elegance.

From *The Book of Cut Flowers* by RP Brotherston (1906)

Containers

The tallish glass vase continued to be the most popular container for flowers. Cut glass, another status symbol, was used both as vases and bowls. Coloured glass took many forms, including beautiful metallic and mottled effects, achieved by Art Nouveau designers. See work by René Lalique, Emile Galle, Louis Tiffany and the Daum brothers. Wedgewood enjoyed a revival.

The following were also used:

Styles and shapes of containers

- Leedsware ceramic baskets and vases
- silver rose bowls, silver trumpet shaped vases with fluted tops
- Art Nouveau vases in ceramics decorated with flowers and leaves or bee, butterfly and dragonfly motifs, as well as shells, wavy forms, peacocks and peacock feathers, fish and serpents and female forms in swirling draperies
- Wedgewood enjoyed a revival
- pewter jugs, mugs, bowls, especially those with Art Nouveau motifs
- copper jugs and Indian brassware of all kinds

Tall glass vase with roses – Charles Rennie Mackintosh, Glasgow (1901)

Arrangement from a contemporary photograph by FG Tutton

Mechanics

Various devices and systems were used, such as glass or pottery 'roses' with holes to hold stems, wet sand, moss; specimen vases for one flower; wire mesh; mesh covers for rose bowls, etc.; strips of lead folded zig-zag fashion in the bottom of a bowl.

Gertrude Jekyll suggests – "a few stiff twigs of box or holly, or bits of spray from an old birch broom" or "a two-tier framework of wire netting".

Suggested accessories

- beads, brooches, buckles and pendants
- Celtic style dress ornaments
- fans – lace, ivory, mother-of pearl
- jet trimmings, sequins
- jewel caskets
- beaded bags
- comb and hair ornaments
- feather boas, ostrich and peacock feathers
- Japanese paper sunshades, parasols
- hand mirrors, hat pins, powder compacts and cigarette cases
- veils

References and resources

Plant material

King Edward VII's favourite flower was said to be *Lathyrus odoratus*, though *Dianthus* are very typical of the period. The most popular are listed below. Queen Alexandra, when Princess of Wales, is quoted as having 'large vases of common beech in the drawing room at Marlborough House' and blossom was brought indoors to be forced and used in simple naturalistic arrangements. Not many of the Edwardian roses are available today, but the taste of the period was for big cabbage blooms – *Rosa* x *centifolia*.

Flowers
Chrysanthemum sp.
Convallaria majalis
Dahlia sp.
Dianthus caryophyllus
Gypsophila sp.
Jasminum sp.
Lathyrus odoratus
Lilium sp.
Myosotis sp.
Narcissus sp.
Orchis sp.
Paeonia sp.
Rosa sp.
Viola sp.

Flowers used in Art Nouveau motifs
Acanthus sp.
Argyranthemum frutescens
Calendula sp.
Carlina sp.
Convolvulus sp.
Cnicus sp.
Dipsacus fullonum
Echinops sp.
Fuchsia sp.
Hyacinthoides non-scripta
Iris sp.
Lonicera sp.
Malus blossom
Nasturtium sp.
Onopordon sp.
Papaver sp.
Tulips sp.
Viscum album

Foliage
Arum sp
Asparagus setaceus
Arundinaria sp.
Acer palmatum
Parthenocissus vitacaea
Phoenix sp.
Smilax sp.
Vitis vinifera

Vivid foliage of indoor plants e.g., species of *Caladium*, *Cyclamen*, *Codiaeum* and *Solenostemon* syn. *Coleus*.

Seed heads, berries
Cortaderia selloana
Hedera sp.
Lunaria annua
Papaver sp.
Physalis alkekengi var. *franchettii*
Typha latifolia

Places and things to see

Museums and galleries

Horta Museum (Brussels, Belgium)

Musée de l'École de Nancy (Nancy, France)

V&A Museum (London) for furniture and artefacts

William Morris Gallery (London)

Historic buildings and monuments

Belfast City Hall (Belfast)

Eros in Piccadilly (London)

Harrods Food Hall (London)

Langtry Manor Hotel (Dorset) – built for Lily Langtry by Edward VII

London Coliseum (London)

Old Bailey (London)

Peter Pan statue in Kensington Gardens (London)

Royal Liver Building (Merseyside)

The Playhouse Theatre (London)

The Ritz (London)

Selfridges (London)

Standen House & Garden (West Sussex)

Westminster Cathedral (London)

Places

Bourneville (West Midlands)

Hampstead Garden Suburb (London)

Letchworth (Hertfordshire)

Port Sunlight (Merseyside)

Gardens

Barrington Court (Somerset) for Gertrude Jekyll gardens

Bodnant (North Wales)

Castle Howard (North Yorkshire) for old roses

Compton Acres (Dorset)

Hestercombe House and Gardens (Somerset) for Gertrude Jekyll gardens

Hever Castle (Kent)

Hidcote Manor (Gloucestershire)

Lime Kiln Rosarium, Claydon (Suffolk) for old roses

Nymans (West Sussex)

See also

Spirit of Ecstasy radiator cap on Rolls Royce cars

People to look up

Designers

Antoni Gaudí (1852–1926)
Casa Mila, other buildings and gardens, La Sagrada Familia Cathedral all in Barcelona (Spain)

Hector Guimard (1867–1942)
Castel Béranger, Musée d'Orsay and Metro stations all in Paris (France)

Charles Rennie Mackintosh (1868–1928)
Glasgow School of Art and Willow Tea Rooms in Sauchiehall Street, both in Glasgow (Lanarkshire) and Hill House (Dunbartonshire)

The 1920s and 1930s
1920–1939

DAPHNE VAGG

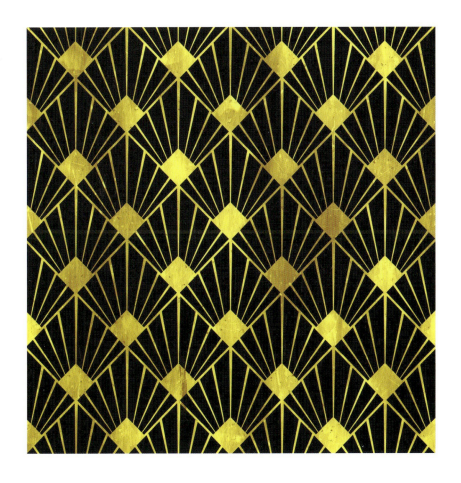

This period between the First and Second World Wars marks the beginning of the so-called modern age and shows a complete break from the Victorian and Edwardian eras which preceded it.

The 1914–1918 war brought about the emancipation of women and the short-skirted, Charleston flapper with bobbed hair of the 1920s who gradually evolved into the sophisticated, Hollywood film star influenced woman of the 1930s. But, the General Strike in 1926, followed by the economic depression of the 1930s, highlighted the contrasting poverty of many, such as miners and mill and factory workers in the aftermath of the Industrial Revolution of the previous century.

In the arts, the Art Deco style with its strongly geometric, rectangular lines and glossy surfaces, influenced the design of buildings, furniture, new electric light fittings, china, ornaments and vases and, those hallmarks of the sophisticated woman – the powder compact and the cigarette case. (The term 'Art Deco' was not actually coined until 1966 but was taken from the International Exhibition of Modern Decorative and Industrial Arts (*Exposition internationale des Arts décoratifs et industriels modernes*) in Paris in 1925. The arrival of Diaghilev's Ballets Russes in the 1920s greatly influenced the use of vivid colours and the 1925 opening of Tutankhamen's tomb started a revival of Egyptian styles and motifs, often seen in the cinemas of the period.

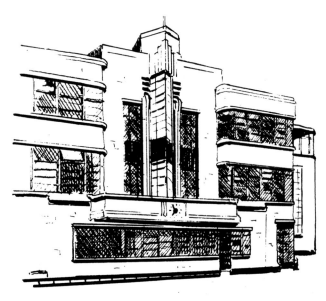

Art Deco style Hoover factory (London)

How and where flowers were used

The use of cut flowers for decoration in homes was general. They were mostly used in a simple, naturalistic manner. In the 1920s, Mrs Beeton, whose work continued to be popular in this period, said "Every flower should be put in the way it grows". Flower arrangements were placed everywhere – on dining tables, hall chests, sideboards, mantelpieces, occasional tables and stools, writing desks, bedside tables, shelves, in fireplaces and on the floor. In the 1930s, spearheaded by Constance Spry, arranging flowers became accepted as an art form and the foundations for the eventual upsurge of flower clubs were laid.

Mrs Beeton advised the use of:

- bowls planted with spring bulbs
- golden autumn beech and oak, pressed bracken, brambles and berries; fresh dark evergreens
- *Physalis alkekengi* var. *franchetii*, dipped in a solution of gum Arabic to last longer
- *Ilex* with plenty of red berries and *Viscum album* at Christmas
- twigs and foliage sprinkled with artificial frost

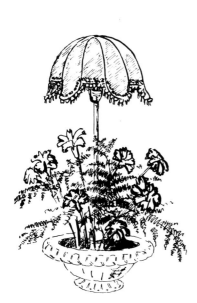

Glass flower bowl with flowers, foliage and a lamp with decorative shade

Paeonia and *Thalictrum* in green glass vase (1920s)

Anne Lamplugh writing in 1929 advised: "You'll put one vase on the floor, won't you? So many flowers are seen at their best from above." (Flower and Vase, London, Country Life Ltd.).
She also recommended:
- miniature gardens in bowls, or simple landscape arrangements especially in spring
- vases of colourful bare twigs, such as willow or dogwood, in winter
- blossom cut in bud to open indoors
- simple colour combinations, for example
- blue and white, mauve and pink, pink and red, plum and copper, apricot and gold, white and yellow, blue and red.

Constance Spry did more than anyone to raise the status of flower arrangement to an art form in the general public's eye.

Her massing of all kinds of plant material, from lichened branches to exotic lilies, cabbages to *Anthurium* blooms, *Nasturtium* to *Laburnum* seedpods and *Hedera* to *Cynara cardunculus*, in a contemporary version of the old Dutch paintings was a revelation. So too was her mastery of colour grouping, either brilliant or subtle as the occasion demanded, and her flair for creating a decoration from a few simple leaves or vegetables is almost legendary. Her first book appeared in 1934 and many more were to follow, taking flower arrangement into the second half of the 20th century.

Constance Spry – mixed bunch in alabaster urn (1934)

Typical settings

- Art Deco glossy surfaces – blackened glass, tinted mirrors, polished brass, chromium plating, patent leather, bright enamels, Bakelite and Vitrolite
- some middle class houses of 'stockbroker Tudor'
- interiors of oatmeal papered walls and grained and varnished woodwork with the wood grain effect combed into the paint.
- combed and stippled plaster walls
- oak was the most favoured wood; at first dark, then medium and light in colour and often limed in the 1930s
- furniture, including the ubiquitous three-piece suite was boxy in outline, with Art Deco mouldings, handles and decoration
- upholstery in uncut moquette and velvet and folk-weave curtains with broad horizontal stripes were popular
- carpets in geometric patterns of orange, yellow, green and blue
- flower patterned wallpapers.

Chrome work table by Legrain

Table decoration

The whole concept of table decoration was changing and it became less formal and more colourful, with white damask going out of favour. Mrs Beeton recommended a lace tablecloth over an underslip to match the colour of the floral decorations or the use of a highly polished table with asbestos mats covered with dainty lace and cut glass or silver candlesticks with shades to match the flower or berries used.

Anne Lamplugh suggests three arrangements for the dining table – one large and high in the centre, flanked by two lower and smaller versions in matching containers.

Constance Spry devoted a whole chapter to table decorations in her first book, seeking to break away from the conventional 'hothouse flowers for the table' even for grander occasions.

A popular table decoration was floating flower heads in a shallow bowl.

Wedding flowers

Wedding bouquets at this time were very large and round with long trails of fern reaching nearly to the ground, almost hiding the bride's dress.

Flowers worn as a corsage were usually limited to one, or at most three flowers with fern. An orchid was the height of sophistication.

Gardens

The development in the 1920s and 1930s of garden cities, large suburban estates of small semi-detached houses led to a great increase in gardening. New home owners, having lived in towns, often had little gardening knowledge, so a kind of standardised plot evolved with a lawn in the middle, a double border, crazy paving and a rockery. The new gardener was ministered by the radio and press. In 1934, the BBC introduced the famous Sunday afternoon *In Your Garden* talks by C H Middleton and there was a rapid growth of gardening magazines.

The increased use of the motor car made garden visiting easier and, in 1927, to take advantage of this newfound habit, the National Gardens Scheme was launched and some 600 gardens opened to the public. Several of our most famous gardens were started, or were in process of creation during the period, such as Westonbirt, Bodnant, Hidcote, Sissinghurst and East Lambrook Manor.

Symbolism

The symbolism of flowers and plants faded into insignificance in this era, save for a few important exceptions:

- **red roses** were still a symbol of love
- **white heather** was still worn for luck
- **red Flanders poppies** became the symbol of remembrance for the dead of the First World War
- **daisies** symbolized the British Empire on which the sun never set (the Empire daisy)

Colour

Colours were either neutrals or strong bright hues.

- **orange** was possibly the most popular colour, but yellow, cobalt blue, viridian green, mauves and purples were all much used
- **red**, both scarlet and crimson, used often with black and silver
- **orange** and green are often teamed together
- **black** lacquer and gleaming silver is typical of sophisticated décor.
- Oatmeal, beige and brown were popular home decoration colours

Containers

- trumpet-shaped glass vases were still used but also bowls and vases in pink, blue or green tinted glass
- pottery posy-rings or troughs, usually in green or beige
- Clarice Cliff pottery
- sturdy unglazed terracotta jugs or pitchers with glazed inside and rim
- brass, copper, pewter bowls, jugs and tankards
- Poole pottery decorated with flowers, especially the stylized Jacobean embroidery type
- the florist's presentation basket with high handle and down-turned brim
- cut-glass rose bowls
- wall pockets or sconces
- shallow bowls in yellow or orange with black inside and a bird ornament, kingfisher or canary, standing in the middle
- tobacco jars, vegetable dishes, honey and salt jars, shells and brown or green painted bread tins
- urns, tazzas, goblets and footed bowls were favoured by Constance Spry

Log-shaped pottery trough

Pottery flower ring with snowdrops

Pewter tankard

Earthenware pitcher

Cut glass rose bowl

Flowers floating in a bowl with black interior and bird decoration

Pottery bowl

Royal Doulton salt glaze vase (1920)

Frosted green glass Art Deco vase

Mechanics

- metal grid covers for vases and bowls, sold complete
- round or rectangular glass 'roses' with holes to hold stems
- strips of inch-wide lead to bend round branches and stems to hold them in place
- stones and chippings
- curved and twisted galvanised or millinery wire
- cut bushy stems and leaves
- Constance Spry used mainly crumpled wire netting

Suggested accessories

- articles in jade, onyx, alabaster, obsidian and crystal
- Art Deco dancing or bathing lady figurines
- plaster or pottery flying ducks in threes on walls
- tableware of geometric shape, triangular saucers, jugs, handles with geometric decoration or painted landscape scenes in orange and green or red and black
- table lamps with shades, often fringed
- cocktail shakers, cigarette cases, ashtrays, powder compacts, lipsticks, long cigarette holders, long strings of beads

Powder compact

Cup and saucer from a 'Tea for Two' set

Cigarette case

A 'new' electric table lamp

Yellow glass cocktail shaker (1936)

Bather with parasol

References and resources

Plant material

Those interested in flower arranging were mainly gardeners, or had gardens. Their lives were generally involved in country pursuits, hence an interest in wild flowers through the seasons, such as primroses, violets, bluebells, ferns, grasses, beech leaves and sticky buds of horse chestnut brought indoors to open.
The following seem especially typical:

Aster amellus
Calendula officinalis
Chrysanthemum sp.
daisy-type flowers
Dianthus caryophyllus
Geranium sp.
Iris foetidissima pods
Nasturtium sp.
Nymphaea sp.
Physalis alkekengi var. *franchetii*

Bowls of fruit were used decoratively and the more adventuresome arrangers were trying out mixed designs of foliage only.

Places to see

Museums and galleries

Brighton Museum & Art Gallery (East Sussex)

Museum of the Home (London)

V&A Museum (London)

Historic buildings and monuments

Castle Drogo (Devon)

The Midland Hotel (Lancashire)

Places

Miami Beach, Florida (USA)

The 1930s' housing estates of any city or town, former cinemas, shopping parades and London Underground stations. Ornaments from the period are now collectors' items.

Useful reading

General flower arranging

A History of Flower Arrangement, Julia S Berrall, (Thames & Hudson, 1969)
A History of Flower Arranging, Dorothy Cooke & Pamela McNicol, (Heinemann, 1989)
Civilisation, Kenneth Clark (John Murray, 2015)
European Flower Painters, Peter Mitchell (A&C Black, 1973)
Flora Domestica: A History of British Flower Arranging 1500-1930, Mary Rose Blacker (The National Trust, 2000)
Flower Arrangements in Stately Homes, Julia Clements (George Newnes, 1966)
Larousse Encyclopedia of Prehistoric & Ancient Art, Rene Huyghe, Editor (Bookthrift Co., 1981)
New Larousse Encyclopedia of Mythology, introduction by Robert Graves, (Hamlyn, 1974)
Period Flower Arrangement, Margaret Marcus (Barrows, 1952)
Still Life, Norbert Schneider (Taschen, 2003)
The Art of Flower Arrangement, Beverley Nichols (Collins, 1967)
The Complete Guide to Flower & Foliage Arrangement, Iris Webb (Webb & Bower, 1979)

Plants and gardens

A Cultural History of Gardens in the Modern Age, John Dixon Hunt, Editor (Bloomsbury Publishing, 2006)
An Illustrated History of Gardening, Anthony Huxley (Paddington Press, first published 1978)
Encyclopaedia of Gardening, T.W. Sanders (W. H. & L. Collingridge, 1931)
Plant Names Simplified New Edition: Their Pronunciation, Derivation and Meaning, AP Stockdale, AT Johnson, et al (5m Publishing, 2019)
RHS Plant Finder (RHS, updated annually)
Royal Horticultural Society Encyclopedia of Plants and Flowers, Christopher Brickell, Editor-in-Chief (Dorling Kindersley, 2019)
The English Pleasure Garden: 1660-1860, Sarah-Jane Downing (Shire Library, 2009)
The Garden: An Illustrated History, Julia S Berrall (Penguin, 1978)
The Hillier Manual of Trees & Shrubs, Roy Lancaster (RHS, 2019)
The Royal Horticultural Society Dictionary of Gardening (Oxford University Press, 1969)
The Story of Gardening: A Cultural History of Famous Gardens from Around the World, Penelope Hobhouse with Ambra Edwards (Pavilion Books, 2019)
The Story of the English Garden, Ambra Edwards (National Trust, 2018)
See also books on the plant hunters of the 18th, 19th and 20th centuries

Historical periods

There are many books on period artefacts, furniture, textiles, silver, porcelain, glass and the decorative arts in general, which will provide useful background details. The internet is also a wealth of information and inspiration as are the websites, social media and printed resources of places of interest, such as relevant museums and historical homes and gardens. The publications listed here reflect the date the *Guide to Period Flower Arranging* was first published (1982). Where known, the most recent editions have been included.

Egypt

All Colour Book of Egyptian Mythology, Richard Patrick (Octopus Books, 1972)
Picture Reference Books No. 14 Ancient Egyptians (Brockhampton Press, 1970)

Greek and Roman

A Dictionary of Roman and Greek Antiquities, Anthony Rich (Longmans, 1893)
Daily Life in Ancient Rome, J Caropine (George Routledge & Sons, 1941)
Everyday Things in Ancient Greece, Marjorie & CHB Quennell (Batsford/Putnam, 1968)
Life in Ancient Athens, TG Tucker (Macmillan 1912)
New Larousse Encyclopedia of Mythology, introduction by Robert Graves (Paul Hamlyn, 1974)
Numerous books on Pompeii and Herculaneum, e.g., *Cities of Vesuvius,* M. Grant (Weidenfeld & Nicholson, 1971)
Pompeii and Herculaneum: The Glory and the Grief, Marcel Brion (Elek Books, 1960)
The Classical World, Donald E. Strong (Paul Hamlyn, 1965)
The Triumph of the Greeks, Paul Wietzel (Paul Hamlyn, 1969)

India

A Brief History of Indian Floral Art, Kavita Poddar (personal document, 2005)
Gardens of Delight: Indian Gardens through the Ages, Rahoul B. Singh (Pavilion, 2008)
Kama Sutra of Vatsyayana (various editions)
Pushpa Aradhana: a Floral Tribute, Amita Prasad and Priyadarshinee Guha (Official World Association of Floral Artists (WAFA) India Floral Art Book, 2019)
Pushpa Bharathi: Flower Arrangements of India, Dhanalakshmi Fordyce (The Perennial Press, 1979).
Saying with Flowers, Uma Basu (currently out of print)
The Life of William Carey, George Smith (John Murray, 1887)
Trees of Delhi: a Field Guide, Pradip Krishnen (Dorling Kindersley, 2006)
See also Pushpa Bitan Friendship Society (Kolkata) pushpabitan.in

Japanese

Classical Ikebana, Georgie Davidson (W.H. Allen/Virgin Books, 1970)
Flower Arrangement: Ikebana Way, William C Steere, Editor (Shufunotomo, 1975)
Ikebana, Takashi Sawano (Littlehampton Book Services Ltd, 1981)
Ikebana: Art of Japanese Flower Arrangement (Barrie & Jenkins, 1976)
Ikebana: Spirit and Technique, Shusui Komoda, Horst Pointer (Cassell Illustrated, 1987)
Masters' Book of Ikebana, John March-Penney (Sampson Low, 1976)
Rikka: Soul of Japanese Flower Arrangement, Yuchiku Fujiwara (Shufunotomo, 1993)
Zen in the Art of Flower Arrangement, Gustie Herrigel (Souvenir Press, 1999)

Chinese

A Short History of Chinese Art,
 Michael Sullivan (Faber & Faber, 1967)
Chinese Art: Recent Discoveries,
 Michael Sullivan (Thames & Hudson, 1973)
Chinese Flower Arrangement, HL Li
 (Dover Publications Inc, 2003)
Chinese Porcelain, Anthony du Boulay
 (Octopus Books, 1973)
Gardens of China, Osvald Siren
 (Ronald Press, 1949) (very informative
 on plants and gardens)
Style, Motif and Design in Chinese Art,
 Michael Ridley (Blandford Press, 1977)
The Chinese Eye, Chiang Lee
 (Methuen, 1936)
*The Chinese Garden: History, Art &
 Architecture*, Maggie Keswick
 (Harvard University Press, 2003)
*The Peking Museum Paintings and
 Ceramics*, François Fourcade,
 Norbert Guterman
 (Thames & Hudson, 1965)
*Treasures of China: Chinese Archaeology
 Since the Cultural Revolution*,
 Michael Ridley (various publishers
 listed, 1973)
World of the Ancient Chinese,
 J.B. Grosier (Magna Books, 1989)

Italian Renaissance

*Daily Life in Florence: In the Time of the
 Medici*, Jean Lucas-Dubreton
 (Routledge, 2021)
Primavera, Umberto Baldini
 (Sidgwick & Jackson, 1986)

Refer to the many paintings from this
period for ideas; the following books
are useful for background information.

The Art of the Renaissance, Peter Murray
 (Thames & Hudson, 1985)
The Renaissance Garden in England,
 Roy Strong (Thames & Hudson, 1979)
The Stones of Florence, Mary McCarthy
 (Mariner Books, 2002)

Tudor

*A History of Everyday Things in England,
 Vol 2 of 2: 1500-1799*, Marjorie Quennell,
 CHB Quennell (Forgotten Books, 2019)
Elizabeth R., Roy Strong,
 Julia Trevalyan Oman
 (Secker & Warburg, 1971)
Flowers and Trees of Tudor England,
 Clare Putnam (Hugh Evelyn, 1972)
Herbs for the Mediaeval Household,
 Margaret B. Freeman
 (Metropolitan Museum of Art, 1971)
Shakespeare's Flowers, Jessica Kerr
 (Johnson Books, 1997)
The Early Tudors at Home,
 Elizabeth Burton (Viking, 1976)
The Elizabethan Woman,
 Carroll Camden (Cleaver-Hume, 1952)
The Elizabethans at Home,
 Elizabeth Burton (Arrow Books, 1973)
The Flowers of Shakespeare,
 Doris Hunt (Magnolia, 1980)
*The Horizon Book of the Elizabethan
 World*, Lacey Baldwin Smith
 (Paul Hamlyn, 1967)
Tudor Family Portrait,
 Barbara Winchester
 (Jonathan Cape 1955)
World of Shakespeare: Plants,
 Alan Dent (Osprey, 1971)

Dutch and Flemish

Paintings for this period are a very rich
source of information and inspiration;
the following books are also useful.

Dutch Flower Painting 1600–1720,
 Paul Taylor, (Dulwich Picture
 Gallery, 1996)
European Flower Painters, Peter Mitchell
 (Interbook International, 1980)

American Colonial

There is little pictorial evidence for flower arranging but the following books may provide inspiration.

American Gardens in the Eighteenth century, Ann Leighton (University of Massachusetts Press, 1987)
An Eighteenth-century Garland, Louisa B. Fisher (Colonial Williamsburg Foundation, 1951)
Chesapeake, James A. Mitchener (The Dial Press, 2013)
Culpeper's Complete Herbal, (originally published 1652, various imprints and editions)
Early English Gardens in New England, Ann Leighton (Littlehampton Book Services, 1970)
Gardens of Colony and State, Alice G. Lockwood, Editor (University of Pennsylvania Press, 2000)
Plants of Colonial Days, Raymond Taylor (Dover Publications, 1997)
The Flower World of Williamsburg, Joan Parry Dutton (Holt, Rinehart and Winston, 1973)
The Winthrop Woman, Anya Seton (Hodder & Stoughton, 2014)

Georgian

Books on furniture, silver, porcelain and glass give useful background information.

A History of British Gardening, Miles Hadfield (Penguin, 1985)
Discovering Period Gardens, John Anthony (Shire Publications, 1997)

Rococo

See the Wallace Collection catalogues, publications, website resources, talks, tours and events for information and inspiration (wallacecollection.org)
The Age of Louis XV - Cameo series (Paul Hamlyn 1969)
The Age of Rococo, Cameo series (Paul Hamlyn)

Victorian

Many books have been and are still being written about Victoriana. Refer to books on art, embroidery, flowers, furniture, fashion, gardening, household matters, pottery and porcelain, Queen Victoria and Prince Albert, the 1851 Exhibition, magazines, diaries and letters generally for period background.

Creating a Victorian Flower Garden, Stephan Buczaki (Collins 1988)
Flowers for Ornament & Decoration, and How to Arrange Them, EA Maling (BiblioLife, 2008, first published 1862)
The Victorian Fern Craze, Sarah Whittingham (Shire Library, 2009)
The Victorians and their Flowers, Nicolette Scourse (Croom Helm, 1983)

Edwardian and Art Nouveau

The V&A Museum is a good starting point for books about Edwardian and Art Nouveau style.
Books produced for the V&A Museum
British Floral Decoration (1910), Robert Forester Felton (Kessinger Publishing, 2010, first published 1910)
Flower Decoration in the House, Gertrude Jekyll (Andesite Press 2017, first published 1907)

1920s and 1930s

Look for books by and about Constance Spry and guides to Art Deco style and the life and work of Clarice Cliff. The following are also useful.

Flower and Vase: A Monthly Key to Room Decoration, Anne Lamplugh (Country Life, 1929)
Mrs Beeton's Family Cookery and Household Management, Isabella Beeton (many editions)

Acknowledgements

NAFAS would like to thank all those who have contributed to this publication. In particular, thanks should go to Alan Beatty, James Burnside and Alwyn Page for checking the botanical names of plants, Margaret Murray for her illustrations in the Indian chapter, Dr Christina Curtis, Ann Harding and the NAFAS Education and Judges Committees for all of their contributions and Pat Stammers for proof reading.

Picture credits

With thanks to the following photographers and photo libraries for permission to reproduce the following images:

Front cover and title page – *A Bouquet of Flowers*, Clara Peeters; Metropolitan Museum of Art, purchase, Lila Acheson Wallace, Howard S. and Nancy Marks, Friends of European Paintings, and Mr. and Mrs. J. Tomilson Hill Gifts, Gift of Humanities Fund Inc., by exchange, Henry and Lucy Moses Fund Inc. Gift, and funds from various donors, 2020

Egyptian: page 9 – GTS Productions/Shutterstock.com

Greek and Roman: page 17 – Yakov Oskanov/Shutterstock.com

Indian: page 25 – saiko3p/Shutterstock.com; page 27 – Macrovector/Shutterstock.com; page 28 (top) – Bhuvanesh S/Shutterstock.com; page 28 (bottom row) – Boo-tique Illustration/Shutterstock.com; page 29 (Om symbol) – VectorPlotnikoff/Shutterstock.com; page 29 (dancers) – Sergei Boshkirov/Shutterstock.com; page 33 (lamp left) – Yevgen Kravchenko/Shutterstock.com; page 33 (lamp right) – Brumgat/Shutterstock.com; page 33 – (Hindu goddess and god) – Irina Simkina/Shutterstock.com

Japanese: page 35 – *Young Ladies Viewing Cherry–blossoms at Asukayama* (detail), Torii Kiyonaga; Metropolitan Museum of Art, H. O. Havemeyer Collection, bequest of Mrs. H. O. Havemeyer, 1929

Chinese: page 45 – cloisonné enamel base for a mandala; Metropolitan Museum of Art, purchase, Florence and Herbert Irving Gift, 1992

Italian Renaissance: page 53 – iStock.com/Vladislav Zolotov

Tudor: page 61 – Linda George/Shutterstock.com

Dutch and Flemish: page 69 – *Flowers by a Stone Vase* (detail), Peter Faes; Museum of Metropolitan Art, bequest of Catherine D. Wentworth, 1948

American Colonial: page 77 – embroidered sampler, Millsent Connor; Metropolitan Museum of Art, gift of Edgar William and Bernice Chrysler Garbisch, 1974; page 81 – Morphart Creation/Shutterstock.com (bottom)

Georgian: page 87 – scent bottle, Josiah Wedgwood; Metropolitan Museum of Art, Rogers Fund, 1908

Rococo: page 97 – VintageStyle/Shutterstock.com

Victorian: page 105 – *Honeysuckle* (detail), William Morris; Metropolitan Museum of Art, Theodore M. Davis Collection, bequest of Theodore M. Davis, 1915

Edwardian and Art Nouveau: page 115 – iStock.com/Montes-Bradley

The 1920s and 1930s: page 125 – iStock.com/itsme23

NAFAS flower clubs

NAFAS-affiliated flower clubs run all over the UK and other countries around the world.
Members enjoy:

- workshops on creating floral designs
- demonstrations from accomplished designers
- entering shows and competitions
- qualification and career opportunities
- fun, friendship and a whole lot more

To find a flower club near you:

 www.nafas.org.uk

 @NafasFlowers

 @nafas_flowerarrangers

The Flower Arranger magazine

The Flower Arranger magazine is the UK's leading floral art magazine published quarterly by NAFAS. Four stunning issues per year packed with:

- international and UK design inspiration
- seasonal step-by-steps
- floral events
- flower news, views and special reader offers.

For up-to-date information and to subscribe visit www.nafas.org.uk Discounted subscriptions are available to Flower Club members – speak to your local representative.

Notes

Notes

Notes

Notes